NOTHING
IS TOO GOOD
TO BE TRUE

JOHN RANDOLPH PRICE

HAY HOUSE, INC.
Carlsbad, California
London • Sydney • Johannesburg
Vancouver • Hong Kong

Published and distributed in the United States by: Hay House, Inc., P.O. Box 5100, Carlsbad, CA 92018-5100 • *Phone:* (760) 431-7695 or (800) 654-5126 • *Fax:* (760) 431-6948 or (800) 650-5115 • www.hayhouse.com • *Published and distributed in Australia by:* Hay House Australia Pty. Ltd., 18/36 Ralph St., Alexandria NSW 2015 • *Phone:* 612-9669-4299 • *Fax:* 612-9669-4144 • www.hayhouse.com.au • *Published and distributed in the United Kingdom by:* Hay House UK, Ltd. • Unit 62, Canalot Studios • 222 Kensal Rd., London W10 5BN • *Phone:* 44-20-8962-1230 • *Fax:* 44-20-8962-1239 • www.hayhouse.co.uk • *Published and distributed in the Republic of South Africa by:* Hay House SA (Pty), Ltd., P.O. Box 990, Witkoppen 2068 • *Phone/Fax:* 27-11-706-6612 • orders@psdprom.co.za • *Distributed in Canada by:* Raincoast • 9050 Shaughnessy St., Vancouver, B.C. V6P 6E5 • *Phone:* (604) 323-7100 • *Fax:* (604) 323-2600

Editorial supervision: Jill Kramer   *Design:* Amy Gingery

The author of this book does not dispense medical advice or prescribe the use of any technique as a form of treatment for physical or medical problems without the advice of a physician, either directly or indirectly. The intent of the author is only to offer information of a general nature to help you in your quest for emotional and spiritual well-being. In the event you use any of the information in this book for yourself, which is your constitutional right, the author and the publisher assume no responsibility for your actions.

Library of Congress Cataloging-in-Publication Data

Price, John Randolph.
 Nothing is too good to be true / John Randolph Price.
 p. cm.
Includes bibliographical references (p.).
 ISBN 1-40190-000-3
       1. New Thought. I. Title.
       BF639 .P852 2003
       299'.93—dc21

                                                    2002009831

ISBN 13: 978-1-4019-0000-7
ISBN 10: 1-4019-0000-3

06 05 04 03   5 4 3 2
1st printing, February 2003
3rd printing, February 2005

Printed in the United States of America

NOTHING IS TOO GOOD TO BE TRUE

Also by John Randolph Price

Books

The Abundance Book
The Alchemist's Handbook
*Angel Energy
*The Angels Within Us
Empowerment
The Jesus Code
*Living a Life of Joy
The Love Book
The Meditation Book
Practical Spirituality
Removing the Masks that Bind Us
A Spiritual Philosophy for the New World
The Success Book
The Superbeings
The Wellness Book
With Wings As Eagles
The Workbook for Self-Mastery

Selected audiocassettes are also available from Hay House

Check your bookstore for the books above. All items except those with
asterisks can be ordered through Hay House:
800-654-5126 • 800-650-5115 (fax)

Please visit the Hay House Website at: **hayhouse.com** and
John Randolph Price's Website at: **quartus.org**

To the New Thought Movement
throughout the world,
and to the Truth that sets us free

Contents

Introduction

To the people of the world, regardless of nationality, ethnic origins, or religion, I say that the time has come to rise from our deep slumber, shake off the dust of frustration and futility, and realize the grandeur that has always been ours. At the very beginning of our existence as a race of beings, we were graced with lavish abundance to meet every need, a perfect body for our adventure in the third dimension, the genius of creative self-expression to contribute to the dignity and beauty of this tangible plane of existence, and the capacity to live conflict-free and enjoy loving relationships with everyone. Then mental darkness slowly descended upon us, and we temporarily lost the consciousness of our magnificent legacy. The sacred became profane.

The gifts of God were given to each one of us as the Divine Design, Heaven's Plan of Completeness, but we went on our way as though our manifest destiny was strife, struggle, and sorrow—God's way of testing our souls. And most of the people on Earth continue to believe in birth and death with little in between to rejoice about. The majority live in fear or poverty, with one form of illness or another, or with inadequate food, clothing, housing, and education. This is certainly *not* the will of God or Heaven's Plan.

Even those of us considered "fortunate" may suffer at times with lack, limitation, sickness, and failure because on some level of mind we've chosen these experiences of darkness. For example, a woman in California told me that she didn't want to be free of a physical malady because then she'd have to go back to work, and her daughter would no longer take care of her. I heard a man in Florida say that he'd lose his friends if he became wealthy, and the money would bring every needy relative to his door. I've also heard from those who believed that an intimate relationship with someone would mean a loss of freedom. And in the opinion of one young woman, success is based on "manipulation and greed." When I asked her what she did for a living, she said, "I do what I have to do to get by."

These choices and attitudes are based on fear and self-ishness and the idea that we have to sacrifice in one area in order to get something in another. Many poor and under-achieving people have found a comfort zone and may not want a different lifestyle. The ones I've known in that category feel that it's their lot in life, just a bad draw from the cosmic deck. "Just getting by" is all they know. But look again from the Divine Perspective: We were *all* created to live rich, full, whole, joyous lives filled with beauty and creative self-expression, and if we're not, we're not fulfilling our destiny.

Yes, there is free will, but how does the one Presence and Power of the universe see this? The light of Truth is eternally shining, the Kingdom is forever given, and nothing is ever withheld because of something called "free will." If we don't accept the gifts, it's only because we don't know that they've been given. It's a state of ignorance—a lack of knowledge, unawareness, confusion—but as the Truth emerges, we see things differently. We become aware that abundance, health, success, and right relations are part of the natural process of life, and as this awareness deepens into understanding, our lives begin to change.

Perhaps another reason for our denial of all that is good, true, and beautiful in life is that we think we have to suffer and atone for past misdeeds. This is nothing more than a faulty interpretation of the law of karma. When we rise into spiritual consciousness, the karmic effects are washed away. Guilt, which demands punishment, dissolves into innocence, and harmony prevails. Or possibly we made an innocent error—

we just didn't understand that we have the creative power to completely change our lives, so we plodded along trying to beat the law of averages.

Then there's the reincarnation rationale. One who is living in the basement of life is released from the physical body and takes a consciousness of lack, illness, loneliness, and strife to the other side. Rather than taking the time for healing, the person makes a quick turnaround and heads back into the Earth plane through an intense desire for objective existence. However, he takes that same state of consciousness along for the ride, and the life may be very similar to the one before. But it doesn't have to be this way. *You shall know the truth, and the truth shall set you free.*

And there are those who have followed the spiritual path for years but still haven't found the true bliss of life. The reason can be attributed to certain beliefs in consciousness, which have roots in religious dogma, family environment, authority figures, or society in general. Trends of thought based on fear, anger, rejection, rebellion, guilt, unworthiness, futility, and unforgivingness have developed into error patterns that hold the person in figurative bondage. But blocks in consciousness can be removed—if the individual is willing to let go of false beliefs and close the door to the past.

EONS AGO, IN AN ATTEMPT TO REAWAKEN HUMANITY, we were given the Divine Design, but the masses weren't ready for the *Fundamental Principle* that would lead them to a state of dignity, nobility, and excellence. The collective consciousness was so hardened that seasons of dying, uprooting, killing, hating, and warring were seen as the only possibilities. But over time, the energy of Truth has silently entered the mainstream of thought, and now there's a crack in that mass of misunderstanding and unbelief. Despite appearances to the contrary, a positive revolution is brewing in minds and hearts—and more and more people are now ready to look differently at their concept of God, themselves, life, and this world. And in the process, antiquated dogmas, religious tyranny, and superstition will be swept away.

It is time.

This book represents a deep probe into that Master Key to life. In Part I, we'll focus on the Grand Paradigm and how to unlock the doors to our Divine Constitution. We'll look at the Secret of the Ages, the bridge to connect Heaven and Earth, the angels within, eliminating blocks in consciousness, and working with the Great Law by directing the cosmic energies and dancing with life. Then we'll bring it all together as Mind into Manifestation and Divine Cause and Divine Effect.

In Part II is the proof of what New Thought can do—the sweet mysteries of life and the fruits of the harvest. "Nothing is too good to be true" is a fact, and miracle will follow miracle when we remove the dam holding back the great river of life and open the blinds that have shut out the light of the shining Truth within. Let's do that, and then spread the word that all things are indeed possible.

The people are waiting for the Good News.

PART I

KEYS TO MASTERY

CHAPTER ONE

The Secret of the Ages

I f we're going to change our lives and return this world to sanity, our first step is to take a close look at the greatest spiritual and philosophical system the world has ever known. This is not an exaggeration. By applying the principles of this system, lives can be dramatically changed. It offers not only hope, but *The Way* to peace, plenty, and a life of true bliss. We call it "New Thought" today, but in reality, it's the Golden Cord of the Perennial Philosophy, the Spiritual Teachings of Ancient Wisdom brought forth as the Secret Doctrine of Practical Mastery. It's the answer to every problem on planet Earth today.

Let's not confuse New Thought with "New Age." The former is a spiritual movement, a divine philosophy, a way of life based in Principle. New Age, on the other hand, is identified with "the Age of Aquarius," based on the motion of the equinoxes, a new period emphasizing freedom and the release from old concepts. It's wonderful that we have this new door of opportunity, but there's so much more to life than an arc of the zodiac. New Age is also a state of mind that focuses on *alternatives*—the unconventional and the nontraditional. There's nothing wrong with that, but in some cases, this has led us into a preoccupation with the world of effects, taking us away from an understanding of Loving *Cause* and giving us many external battles to fight. And in the eyes of many fundamentalists, New Age has been seen as anti-Christian, promoting a one-world religion and government with a vast network of organizations designed to establish a New World Order.

There may be fringe groups that have contributed to this belief with their emphasis on inner governments, the uniting of church and state in an esoteric theocracy, and so-called control conspiracies, but such activities are not in tune with the love, joy, beauty, and purity of New Thought. Personally, I'd like to see us draw from all religions; find our freedom as *individuals* in the mainstream of Right Thinking; take our eyes off "this world" for a time; and focus on God, Truth, and Self-Reliance. As Ralph Waldo Emerson said, "The only progress ever known was of the individual."

To continue, Truth was first given to sleeping humanity in symbols, next in music and song, later in myths and legends, and then in poetry and parables. One of these legends tells us that in 9500 B.C., spiritually illumined Initiates became the first "divine" rulers in Egypt. They were considered the Grand Magicians, having the mind power to manifest form and maintain dominion over the effects of this world. Little else is known about them, and we later pick up their thread in about 5000 B.C., when "Great Ones" appeared to teach the functional principles of cosmic law, the spiritual powers of each individual, and the aspects of God that represent the laws of all phenomena.

The key here was to understand that we create our own reality, that mind is the creative agent, and that we have the power to project either a Heaven or hell on the screen of life. This was the first teaching that dealt with metaphysical principles and what we now call the *subjective realm*—that what we impress on the inner is expressed in the outer. It was also the initial revelation of the causal powers within us, first called *neters* and later referred to as *archetypes*, or original patterns of living energy. These ancient archetypes predate all wisdom teachings in written form, and most aspects of religion, philosophy, astrology, and metaphysics are directly or indirectly based on these causal powers living and working in each individual's energy field.

It was during this time that Freemasonry, the craft of initiated builders, came forth. Albert Pike has written that Masonry is "more ancient than any of the world's living religions," and it was said that through an understanding of spiritual Reality and a dedication to Wisdom, Love, and Service, the Master Masons attained "supernatural" powers. The Rosicrucian Order, with its emphasis on spiritual rebirth and the Law of Love, can also be traced back to this period in history.

In 3000 B.C., we were introduced to the "Twelve Labors of Hercules," a symbolic drama portraying the path of return to Truth. It was a continuing call to "know thyself" as God made manifest. According to *The Labours of Hercules: An Astrological Interpretation,* by Alice A. Bailey:

> . . . back of the objective world of phenomena, human or solar, small or great, organic or inorganic, lies a subjective world of forces which is responsible for the outer form. Behind the outer material shell is to be found a vast empire of BEING. . . . Everything outer and tangible is a symbol of inner creative forces and it is this idea that

underlies all symbology. A symbol is an outer and visible form of an inner and spiritual reality.

It is with this interplay of the outer form and the inner life that Hercules wrestles. He knew himself to be the form, the symbol, for the dominance of the lower material nature made its presence felt with the facility of age-long expression. At the same time he knew that his problem was to express spiritual being and energy. He had to know in fact and in experience that he was God, immanent in nature; that he was the Self in close relation to the Not-Self; he had to experiment with the law of cause and effect, and this from the standpoint of the initiator of the causes in order to produce intelligent effects."[1]

When the 12 labors were completed, Hercules's teacher said, "The jewel of immortality is yours. By these twelve labors have you overcome the human, and put on the divine. Home you have come, no more to leave."[2]

Think now. In the far distant past, it was taught that we are spiritual beings endowed with all the powers of God, and as we overcome the human, we have dominion over this world. Within 500 years of this myth, mystics in ancient India began receiving and spreading the Truth that God is All, and the Self is God, God alone the Reality of all beings.

Then, between 2500 and 1500 B.C. (the dates vary), Hermes Trismegistus, the "scribe of the gods," came on the world stage to tell about the Spirit of the Divine within. In his writings, he implores humanity to "rise from your sleep of ignorance" and to find the Light. He tells us that we have the power to partake of immortality when we *change our minds*, and he gave us the Seven Hermetic Principles as the way to mastery. They are as follows:

1. The Principle of Mentalism: There is but one Mind, one Power, all Divine. We use the same mind and power in our individual worlds that the All did in creating the universe.

2. The Principle of Correspondence: As above, so below. This shows us that there is a correspondence or analogy existing between things spiritual and things physical—the same laws operate in each realm. This is truly the secret of manifestation.

3. The Principle of Vibration: In each energy field, there is a vibration of either attraction or repulsion based on the trend of thoughts. These thoughts are both conscious and unconscious, and on each level, creative action is taking place.

4. The Principle of Polarity: Polarity is to think and feel in a certain direction, to bring our thoughts in tune with Infinite Mind, which forms a path for the flow of the divine energy. It is living life according to our highest truth.

5. The Principle of Rhythm: Life is like a pendulum, a swinging back and forth. When we understand this principle, we polarize ourselves at the point of optimum living, thus neutralizing the ups and downs of life.

6. The Principle of Cause and Effect: Every cause has its effect; every effect has its cause; everything happens according to Law. Chance is but a name for the Law not recognized. As a man thinketh in his heart, so is he.

7. The Principle of Gender: Each individual is both male and female, mind and feelings, objective and subjective, the I and the Me. What the mind impresses on the feeling nature is manifest in the phenomenal world.

In 1335 B.C., Moses brought his esoteric teachings from Egypt in the Exodus. According to Manly P. Hall, "Moses was an accredited representative of the secret schools, laboring—as many other emissaries have labored—to instruct primitive races in the mysteries of their immortal souls. . . . The word *Moses*, when understood in its esoteric Egyptian sense, means one who has been admitted into the Mystery Schools of Wisdom and has gone forth to teach the ignorant concerning the will of the gods and the mysteries of life, as these mysteries were explained within the temples of Isis, Osiris, and Serapis."[3]

Zoroaster appeared in 628 B.C., to be known as the Persian prophet who taught the truth of the one and only God, a Supreme Being of Good Thought, Beauty, Holiness, Righteousness, Perfect Health, Dominion, and Immortality. Zoroaster believed in the oneness of God and individual being, and that prayers were the "speaking of friend to friend."

Lao-tzu incarnated in 604 B.C., later to found the Taoist religion in China, with its emphasis on living in harmony with the great Universal Impersonal Power. He taught that Heaven, Earth, and man/woman were all created to be in harmony with one another, but we lost our way and miscreated a world of disharmony.

We move on now to about 600 B.C., when Pythagoras—a Mason, and also considered to be the world's first philosopher—was born. He founded a Mystery School at Crotona in Southern Italy, and his teachings reveal another important thread in the Golden Cord of the Perennial Philosophy, an ancient truth carried forward to this day. Pythagoras taught that God, or Supreme Mind, was the Cause of all things, and since God was all Truth, then the effect of this Cause must be Truth, or Spiritual Reality—

when the individual was in harmony with Cause. He believed that we needn't ask for anything because the Intelligent Power of God was eternally providing all things necessary. Thus, the "secret" of prayer was to be in tune with Infinite Mind.

In 563 B.C., Siddhartha Gautama came forth to become Buddha, the Enlightened one. He believed in universal good will expressed from a heart of love "that knows no anger, that knows no ill will." Gautama understood that lack, limitation, disease, and death are but *illusions,* not created by God, therefore not real. His Eightfold Path to freedom encompassed right belief, right aspiration, right speech, right action, right livelihood, right effort, right thought, and right meditation. As a true New Thought statement, he said, "All that we are is the result of what we have thought. If a man speaks or acts with an evil thought, pain follows him. If a man speaks or acts with a pure heart, happiness follows him, like a shadow that never leaves him."

In 427 B.C., the Greek philosopher Plato entered the Earth plane. At the age of 49, he was initiated into the Greater Mysteries, the initiation taking place in the Great Pyramid of Egypt. In 397 B.C., he opened a school called the *Academy,* which became the first university in the history of Europe. H. P. Blavatsky wrote: "Basing all his doctrines upon the presence of the Supreme Mind, Plato taught that the *nous,* spirit, or rational soul of man, being 'generated by the Divine Father,' possessed a nature kindred, or even homogeneous, with the Divinity, and was capable of beholding the eternal realities.[4]

Plato put great emphasis on the *Ideal Life* as a goal toward which people should work. This "Ideal" means that every individual is worthy of a royal life of beauty and nobility—that nothing is impossible to "Gods in Expression." He also introduced the *Christos:* the immortal Self endowed with all the qualities of Deity.

Then we had the Master Jesus, an Essene. He was introduced to us in the New Testament, and his statements of

Truth continue to shine through the pages. However, as a whole, these books of the Bible, which weren't finalized until nearly A.D. 400, must be interpreted esoterically. As we shall see, they've been rewritten numerous times to prove the church's point of view; yet secretly, enlightened ones have contributed their part and have provided coded instructions reflecting the teachings and philosophy of the earlier Masters. Jesus, the Master of the Law of Love, is shown to be the representative of everyone, our brother in the universal family of God, a Model for our completeness—spiritually, mentally, emotionally, and physically.

Continuing the "New Thought" Golden Cord, we're told that we are *the light of the world,* that we *must be perfect* as a fact of life, that we are to *heal the sick, raise the dead, cleanse the lepers, cast out demons* because *all things are possible.* This is true, for *the kingdom of God is in the midst of you. Ye are gods* and *the Spirit of truth dwells with you, in you. You yourself are full of goodness, filled with all knowledge,* for you *have received, not the spirit of the world, but the spirit which is from God. Christ in you, the hope of glory. You are of God.*

In the Pistis Sophia Treatise of the Gnostics, Jesus takes it even further: "Do ye still not know and are ye ignorant? Know ye not and do ye not understand that ye are all Angels, all Archangels, Gods, and Lords, all Rulers, all the great Invisibles, all those of the Midst, those of every region of them that are on the Right, all the Great Ones of the emanations of the Light with all their glory . . . "[5]

The truth was clearly expressed, and with this remembering in minds and hearts, the powers were again released. In the *Decline and Fall of the Roman Empire,* Edward Gibbon reports that during the first century, the lame walked, the blind saw, the sick were healed, the dead were raised, and the laws of nature were frequently suspended.

But it all changed. In A.D. 180, Irenaeus, Bishop of Lyons, attacked independent thinking and all teachings relating to the oneness of God and man. Believing that a spiritual consciousness and a personal union with God would undermine the authority of the priests, he directed his wrath upon Gnosticism. First he issued his *Five Books Against Heresies,* followed by a list of acceptable writings—choosing only those words that supported his demand for a fixed dogma. The shift in mind-direction from within to without had begun, and the innate power of the individual was gradually given to an outer structure and a lower authority.

When emperor Theodosius made Christianity the sole and official religion of the state in A.D. 395, the Institution assumed complete control over individual minds and humanity entered the thousand-year period referred to as *the Dark Ages.* The feudal system controlled secular life, and the keys to spiritual enlightenment were held by the church leaders. A too-free subjective interpretation of the doctrine, or lack of faith in the state religion, resulted in extreme penalties. And with the constant struggle between the church and the individual, the mastery techniques dealing with freedom from need and the science of forces and forms were temporarily lost. The Western mind was kept "in the dark" until the institutional structure began to crack in the 1500s . . . and the eternal principles of oneness and unity began to resurface.

In Europe in the 1600s, the Rosicrucian Fraternity surfaced again and became the center of philosophical discussion. Members of this secret society were known to transcend the limitations of the physical world through their spiritual awakening. They taught that within each individual being was the Supreme Secret of the universe, and that by following the Path of Reality, Truth shall be revealed.

Other secret societies based on the teachings of the Greek Mystery Schools also emerged in England, France, and

Germany; and in the 1800s, the philosophical movement known as *transcendentalism* came into full bloom as the beginning of New Thought in America. The writings of Ralph Waldo Emerson played a significant role in advancing the ancient teachings of Truth. He wrote: "Let us stun and astonish the intruding rabble of men and books and institutions by a simple declaration of the divine fact. Bid them take the shoes from off their feet, for God is here within." Emerson, who had studied the Ancient Mysteries, knew that once these eternal Truths are appropriated by mind, we're no longer controlled by fate. We pass into a *higher council chamber* and a life of sovereignty.

Emerson said, "Place yourself in the middle of the stream of power and wisdom which animates all whom it floats, and you are without effort impelled to truth, to right and a perfect contentment." To him, prayer was not to "effect a private end" but to establish oneness with God in consciousness and then see the miraculous activity of God at work.

Next came the Metaphysical Movement ushered in by Phineas Quimby, the Theosophical Society founded by H. P. Blavatsky and Henry Olcott, and Christian Science founded by Mary Baker Eddy. And then the New Thought Movement came forth through the work and teachings of Charles and Myrtle Fillmore (Unity), Nona Brooks (Divine Science), and Ernest Holmes (Religious Science). While appreciating the philosophies of the religious-metaphysical organizations that preceded it, the New Thought pioneers didn't fully accept their doctrines with such emphasis placed on karma and "mortal mind." The idea that there's no truth, reality, or substance in objective appearances was also quickly dismissed, thus paving the way for greater understanding of Mind and manifestation. There are no "mesmeric illusions." All is Universal Mind "pressing out" into visibility as the substance of all things. Now the principle for health, wealth, and happiness was complete.

In *A Holmes Reader on Meaning,* Ernest Holmes wrote:

The Bible says that in the beginning all things were made by the Word and without the Word was not anything made that is made. It also says that the Word became flesh and dwelt among us. This strikes at the very bottom of spiritual philosophy, emphasized by Jesus and Plato, Swedenborg, Buddha, Whitman, Browning and others, in which they affirm that for every objective, physical or material fact in the universe there must be a subjective, spiritual or mental cause which is the power and reality back of the fact.

The universe is a spiritual system, conceived in the Mind of God as an idea, and automatically projected into manifestation through mental and spiritual laws. Browning said that we should release the "imprisoned splendor," which is the divine pattern within us. Whitman said, "I doubt not that there are other eyes behind these eyes." Swedenborg taught a law of correspondences; that the invisible world contains a pattern of everything in the visible. We find the same teaching in the philosophy of Plato and his followers, in which they say there is a prototype or likeness in the invisible world for everything that appears in the visible.[6]

In another booklet, Holmes wrote:

That which distinguishes the new thought from the old is not a denial of this Divine Reality, but an affirmation of its immediate availability. The miracles of the ages must become commonplace occurrences in the new order of life. The lightning which flashed across the heavens and frightened primordial man with the terror of its magnificence, is some part of that same electrical energy which

drives our modern world. The awfulness of God which
struck terror into the hearts of our ancestors is today the
benign Power, the gentle Influence, and the persistent
Law which governs our thought.

Let us convert prayer into a conscious communion with
the Invisible and faith into a dynamic use of spiritual
Power. Let us take the "mist" out of the mysterious. Let us
understand that one Divine Power has always existed and
has always interpreted Itself to people by interpreting
Itself through them.[7]

In 1915, William Walker Atkinson gave us a brief history
of New Thought. Here are excerpts from his book *New
Thought: Its History and Principles:*

In 1840, *The Dial* was founded, with Margaret Fuller
as the first editor, and such men as Emerson, Channing,
Alcott, Theodore Parker, Ripley, and Thoreau, as con-
tributors. Afterwards, Emerson became the editor. This
journal was the official organ of the Transcendental Movement, and served to fasten the attention of the nation upon
it and its principles.

New Thought is not an organization—it is a MENTAL
ATTITUDE. Many manifest "New Thought" principles
with success in their everyday lives—and yet do not realize that New Thought has had anything to do with their
views. They have simply *absorbed* the New Thought spirit
which surrounds them on all sides. The orthodox pulpits
echo New Thought sermons every Sunday, although the
term is never mentioned—and this, too, is well, for New
Thought is, and should be, as free as air, and the property
of all. . . . And now for a brief statement of the general principles of New Thought. . . .

The fundamental principle underlying all New Thought ideas is that there exists AN INFINITE AND ETERNAL SPIRITUAL PRINCIPLE OF BEING. This Principle of Being . . . is without beginning and without ending; without limits of time, space, or power; absolute; unconditioned; and alone without a second, a rival, or a companion. The qualities of Omnipotence, Omnipresence, and Omniscience—all power, all-presence, and all-wisdom—are attributed to it.

This Principle of Being is regarded as non-material and spiritual in its nature. It is thought of as Pure SPIRIT. The essence of Spirit being regarded as MIND, the Principle of Being is spoken of as Universal Mind. Its substance is regarded as Mental Substance. Its power is regarded as Mental Power. From this arises the statement that 'All is Mind,' including the manifestation, emanation, or expression, of Mind.

This Principle of Being is held to be ONE and one only. There being nothing in existence other than this One Principle, the universe must be regarded as necessarily an emanation, manifestation, or expression of the One Principle of Being. And, we, being a part of the universe, must also be an emanation, expression, or manifestation of that One Principle of Being. There is nothing else for us to be. Moreover, the One Principle of Being must be *immanent* in everything, in different degrees of expression and manifestation.

Therefore, in the degree that man is able to express and manifest this indwelling power must be his individual power. There is no other power to be; no other place from which it may be drawn. From this arises the simple but clear definition of New Thought: *"The recognition, realization, and manifestation of the God in me."*

New Thought holds that our mental states, attitudes, ideas, images, and actions determine our mental and physical conditions and status. . . . Not only is our character the result of our thoughts, but so also is our environment, our health, our physical condition, our degree of success and attainment.

Health, Happiness, and Prosperity belong to man by right, and may be realized by his recognition, realization and manifestation of the Principle within him, by the proper exercise of his mental powers. Here then we find what makes the New Thought *new*. It is the practical application of these world-old truths. (New Thought) has harnessed the spiritual forces, just as it has the material forces, and pressed them into service in the affairs of man. It has placed within the hands of man the machinery for working out his own destiny—for mastering his own fate. It has discarded the old idea that man is a "worm of the dust," a creature of Fate, and a pawn of Circumstance. It bids him lift his head and gaze with unfaltering eyes upon the universe saying: I am the Captain of my Soul, the Master of my Fate, the Ruler of Circumstances![8]

Contemplations

Perhaps the primary focus of what I call "New Thought" can be found in these contemplations:

There is a Presence and Power within me. It is all-knowing, all-caring, all-loving, all-powerful. It is the Completeness of the universe individualized as me. It is who I am. It is what I am. It is God as me now.

God IS. God is the one universal Presence and Power, the Cosmic Heart of Love, expressing as all that is good, true, and beautiful in life. I am that Expression. I and the Spirit of God are one. I am God being me, and God loves Itself as me.

CHAPTER TWO
The Missing Link

The "old thought" of limited religious teachings created a separation between God and the individual, whereas "New Thought" established eternal oneness. This isn't a condemnation of religion as a whole, for to some extent it has contributed to the advancement of civilization. Yet if the so-called great religions had revealed and taught the missing link—*God is expressed AS each individual man and woman*—conditions of ignorance, poverty, starvation, disease, and oppression wouldn't be so prevalent in the world today.

We could say that the religious zealots and fanatics, past and present, are the ones who have veiled the true teachings. Emerson wrote, "It is not wise, not natural, to belong to any religious party." It was his belief that "historical Christianity has fallen into the error that corrupts all attempts to communicate religion." The same could be said for other religions through their misunderstanding of the Wisdom Teachings, which resulted in beliefs emphasizing victimization, divine vengeance, the sorrows of existence, and passive fatalism.

Emerson also said that "America shall introduce a pure religion"—and what could be purer than an understanding of the oneness of God and all creation? The light of this Truth is beginning to penetrate the darkness, and although the subjugation and disempowerment of women continues throughout the world, the modern-day mystics and enlightened thinkers in most religious bodies are working to restore the missing link. And as the understanding of this equality of oneness broadens, it won't be long before religious hardliners soften their stance on intolerance, persecution, and prejudice, and the world will return again to sanity.

The missing link is truly the bridge to connect Heaven and Earth:

The one Presence and Power of the universe is individualized as me now. There is no separation between me and God, for I am God in full and glorious expression. God, the infinite Consciousness of the universe, expresses Itself as me, as everyone. If Consciousness expresses Itself, what is Its expression? Consciousness. Consciousness expresses as consciousness, Mind as mind, Spirit as spirit, Life as life, God as God.

There is only one Identity. God is all there is. If it is not of God, it does not exist. I am of God, and it is impossible for there to be anything unlike God in, through, and as me.

I am the Allness of God in unique expression.
All of God is where I am. God is what I am.

I realize that the "human" mind, emotions, and body have all been negatively identified as the *ego*—that is, something separate and apart from God—but this isn't what the Masters have taught for eons. *God and I are One* was the central message. As Jesus put it, referring to the Spirit or fathering energy within, "All that the Father is, I am; All that the Father has, is mine." He wasn't speaking exclusively from or as the Divine Consciousness—he was speaking as a man. We must understand that we aren't just a man or woman with a body, mind, and emotions, overshadowed by a spiritual Presence, a Holy Self. No, we are that Presence as the All of us.

MY FRIEND WALTER STARCKE, author of *It's All God* and other fine books, has written:

> When you are free of egotism, yet also free of self-denial, you are ready to take your place as God's personalized presence on earth, and the time has come for anything that tempts you to feel "it is robbery to be equal with God" to be recognized and done away with.
>
> By their very nature teachings imply that if you follow their directions you will become something that you are not now already being. Even when they tell you that you are an expression of God, often there is a denial because there is an implication that the 'you' that is in the world is other than your impersonal God-Self. Even the teachings that embody the I AM as a mystical possibility blindside the experience by making it future and by implying it will take place when the personal level no longer exists.
>
> Trying to eliminate all personal sense has not only lured people into futile years of fruitless and disappointing religious discipline, but the belief that the personal self is other than the I AM has assured failure.

The impersonal Self is expressing itself AS your personal being, and in doing so it is no less divine. The Word is made flesh but it is still the Word. The impersonal you has become the personal you, but it is still impersonally expressing itself; so until and unless you honor your personal self, you cannot honor God, your impersonal source.[1]

Yes, until we truly understand the missing link, the *All-Is-God* teaching could certainly backfire. Imagine the consequences if we all went around telling people we were God. And someone spiritually immature with their mental/emotional shoes on backwards could very well wreck havoc with such an idea. There must be a deep awareness, understanding, and knowledge of this Truth—that the personal self is no less spiritual than Absolute Being. And when this dawning takes place, there will be no need to talk about it. By your fruits, people will know you.

Contemplations

The only power is of God, and from the heart of Universal Being to the heart of individual being is the unity of Spirit, for God cannot be separated from God.

I am the Self-Expression of my Universal Mind. As above, so below.

God is in expression AS me in the physical world. As within, so without.

As God being me, I have the consciousness of abundant supply. It has been here all the time, waiting to be recognized. I feel the living flame of wealth in my heart and see it spreading throughout my world as perfect all-sufficiency.

As the Presence of God, I have the consciousness of radiant health and wholeness. This Truth stirs my feeling nature with joy and gladness. I know now that there is nothing to fear.

My personal self is the expression of the Spirit of success, and the consciousness of glorious achievement and accomplishment is outpicturing in the phenomenal world.

God is as me now, which means that the consciousness of love anchored in my heart is attracting perfect relationships to me now. I let my consciousness be the mighty magnet.

I love the God-Self I AM with all my being, and I love the expression of my Self as me. The God of Heaven has become the God of Earth, forever One in Mind and Manifestation.

I am the Light of the Lord, the transmitter of substance to create form and experience, the holy expression of my God Self. I am the Mind of Personal Identification, and I am blessed with the treasures of Heaven.

CHAPTER THREE
Our Divine Constitution

To fully understand the *God-Is-All* Truth, think of infinity—without beginning or end. Think of Omnipresence, God present in all places at the same time. Contemplate infinite, omnipresent Universal Mind. As you do, you're eliminating the concept of space, for there's no such thing as nothingness, void, blank, omission. All that *IS* is filled by *ALL* That Is. Ponder the idea that you live, move, and have your being in Universal Mind, in a sea of infinite, intelligent Substance.

Within this Universal Mind are the masculine and feminine aspects of Father-Mother God—the *Knower* and the *Doer*—Mind and the activity of Mind. This unity of the Absolute and the Creative, everywhere present in distinct vibrations, expresses as innumerable energy fields of individual beings. The *Knower* remains in the Absolute, in a state of Fourth-Dimensional Consciousness—unconditional, pure, complete. The *Doer*, in a vibration suitable for manifestation in the world of form (third dimension), permeates and activates the individualized energy field with its intelligent Substance. You are a force field of this focused energy as physical plane man-woman, the *Chooser*, a pool of consciousness, aware of both the invisible God-Mind and the visible objective world of energy in form. Remember that all is Mind in different rates of vibration.

Slowly contemplate the following. Stretch your mind. Feel the expansion of consciousness.

GOD *IS* . . .

Mind filling all space.
Spirit filling all space.
Substance filling all space.
Truth filling all space.
I AM filling all space.
Energy filling all space.
Light filling all space.
Cause filling all space.
Life filling all space.
Love filling all space.
Will filling all space.
Power filling all space.
Intelligence filling all space.
Wisdom filling all space.
Wealth filling all space.
Success filling all space.
Perfection filling all space.
The *ALL* filling all space, everywhere present.
Lack does not exist.

GOD APPEARS *AS* EVERYTHING . . .

As the Substance-energy of all form and experience:

- The Mineral Kingdom
- The Plant Kingdom
- The Animal Kingdom
- The People Kingdom
  1. Money
  2. Perfect Body
  3. Creative Self-expression
  4. Right Relations
  5. Guidance and Protection
  6. Peace
  7. Joy
  8. Divine Order
  9. As All that could be desired as effect.

See your conscious mind as a ring of light in an infinite realm of Light. There is no separation from your Source and that which God *is*, and appearing *as*. There is no place where God leaves off and something else begins. Around and within the ring is the same endless Light. You're one forever with the *Knower* and the *Doer*.

THE *KNOWER* IS UNIVERSAL MIND *BEING* GOD IMMANENT. It's Fourth-Dimensional Mind, and in this Mind, there's no idea or thought of lack, limitation, conflict, sickness, or failure. It's the Source of everything we could possibly desire in life, forever in a state of completion. It's the domain of Absolute Truth.

This Aspect of God radiates Its Knowingness of individual perfection as Truth. This Living Truth includes the Divine Vision that sees you as totally fulfilled in life mentally, emotionally, and physically. There are no problems that haven't already been solved, no challenges to overcome, no needs that haven't been met. The Knowing Vision is one of lavish abundance, a flawless physical system, ideal relationships, and fulfilling creative self-expression. Nothing is missing for a whole, complete, and joyous life.

> *Dismiss all concepts and images of God as an entity separate and apart from you, or as a demander of justice and punishment, a jealous master, an angry ruler, or as one who must be petitioned for gifts, favors, and divine doles. God is absolute goodness, total givingness, does not know the concept of sin or punishment, has created a universe of beauty for Itself, and has expressed as your individual Divine Consciousness—your kingdom of peace and plenty where life is to be enjoyed to the fullest.*

PAUSE FOR A MOMENT and contemplate this Presence of God you are. Think of Omniscience—all-wisdom, all-knowing— and feel this divine energy pouring through your crown chakra. Think of Omnipotence, the one power, and realize you are that power. This Omnipresent Spirit is pure unconditional love— feel the love pouring into your heart. It is perfect life. Feel this life force animating your physical body. See yourself now as Spirit sees you. The Vision is one of completeness—a perfect body, financial plenty, ideal relationships, and fulfilling creative achievement. Since that's the Vision above, it must be true below. As above, so below.

This one Presence and Power is the Father-Mind of Perfection in Ancient Wisdom; the One that is Everything to Pythagoras—the refuge, strength, fortress, shield and buckler, light and salvation, deliverer, and King of glory of the Psalms; and the Lord of Heaven and Earth to Jesus. It is God *as* you. Accept this Truth now with deep feeling.

THE *DOER* IS CREATIVE MIND, THE ACTIVITY OF GOD. It's the Feminine Principle of our being, the Me of Hermes, the Divine Mother-Substance of the Ancients, the subjective realm of metaphysics. As impersonal Law operating on the plane of the third dimension, the Divine Feminine takes our thoughts, feelings, beliefs, and convictions, and creates corresponding forms and experiences in the phenomenal world.

Scientists tell us that light is energy, producing hundreds of trillions of vibrations per second in the form of light waves. Consider now that the Source of Light is Divine Intelligent Substance, and that the light waves are eternally emanating through your consciousness as lines of force. These lines of force govern electrons and cause atoms to cluster in an energy field as a *thoughtform*. This energy configuration is then "stepped down" to become visible on the physical plane. Everything considered "matter"—whether visible or invisible—is made up of atoms, of pure energy. Therefore, everything seen or unseen is energy in motion. The computer I'm typing this manuscript on is pure energy, God "standing under" (the substance of) the visible appearance. Money, the physical body, creative success, and right relations are nothing less than God in expression. To understand this is to comprehend Mother-Substance as the creating and attracting principle of all form and experience.

We are what we think about all day long, and if we're experiencing any form of discord, scarcity, sickness, or failure, it's because we've planted these seed thoughts in the fertile soil of our Creative Mind. Same thing with our emotions—deep feelings are *always* impressed on the Great Law of our being, and are then carried forth into physical-material experiences. Feelings/emotions of anger, vengeance, and resentment— or images of disaster, poverty, and sickness—branded on the impersonal power will bring about such conditions. And when words accompany the negative feelings and images, unhappy situations are sure to follow.

My energy field is the intelligent Substance of God being me. I will plant only seeds of love, harmony, and truth in my Creative Mind. I will be vigilant, the watchman at the gate, assuring that only thoughts and feelings of the highest order will be impressed upon the Great Law of my being.

THE *CHOOSER* IS THE FATHER-MOTHER SPIRIT expressed in the third dimension (the manifest world of effects) as our personal consciousness. This soul, or *sun* (as it was originally spelled), completes the trinity of Being. Think of an egg-shaped energy field filled with, and supported by, Spirit/Substance. Within this field are the masculine-feminine Energies as one beholding Itself from a different vibration of Mind, for there is only one Mind—universal and individual. However, there are many levels of personal consciousness, all of which influence our emotions and behavior, and this includes the shining light of Truth within, that part of the soul that knows itself as God in expression. From this united force field of mind comes the personality. Many times we put down this phase of mind as an instrument of ego, yet Ernest Holmes has said that "to know that one is the personality of God is the beginning of wisdom."

Originally, the Knowingness of Spirit so filled our conscious minds that we lived as the "Light of the Lord." This observer aspect was continually fed the energy of Truth, and was the transmitter of the Divine Ideals to Creative Mind to manifest perfect forms and conditions in the external world. But over time, through a primary identification with what we thought was a "material" world, we temporarily lost our conscious awareness of our true nature. Even though the eternal flame of Truth continued to burn within, a form of amnesia consumed the mental body. When this state of mind prevails, the natural inclination is to develop a new identity. This is how and when the human ego, a false belief, was formed. Then we began to create selfishly, and competition was born. Destruction followed, and protection from destruction. Self-preservation became our basic instinct, followed by wars and the concept of death, which was not a part of the Divine Plan.

We are where we are today according to our belief system, but as the Masters have said for centuries, it's never too late to change our minds—to restore personal consciousness to its rightful place in the trinity of our being where *nothing is too good to be true.*

> *I am a spiritual being, a single Identity ever perfect and complete. I was not created as a separate being, for God does not know other than Itself. God is Consciousness, and it is only Consciousness that expresses individually. I am consciousness. I have no mind of my own, for there is only one Mind; no mortality exists, no separate being, only the One which I am. All is Spirit.*

WE LOOK ABOVE AND OPEN OURSELVES to the Reality of our lives—the *Knowingness* of perfection. In this Supermind, the Great I AM, there's only the consciousness of unlimited abundance, total fulfillment, absolute wholeness, and eternal harmony—the Truth. I realize that it may be difficult to be centered in Truth, in spiritual consciousness, moment by moment, but we must make the effort to govern our thoughts, manage our emotions, control our words, and imagine only what we wish to have manifest in our lives. That which we cast upon the waters of life will surely return to us in one way or another. Let's also remember that what we wish for another out of anger and vengeance, we're wishing for ourselves. Why become a magnet for conflict?

Now, in your mind, feel the three Aspects of your Being: the *Knower*—God Immanent, the Universal Mind of Love individualized; the *Doer*—Spirit as Law, the one Universal Mind in a vibration of Mother Substance, flowing Life, shining Light, radiating Energy; and the *Chooser*—personal consciousness, the Whole Spirit in focused expression as our soul in tune with Truth. It's through personal consciousness that the Light-Substance flows, going before us to appear as whatever we're holding in mind. The *Knower, Doer,* and *Chooser* are one!

Close your eyes now and contemplate your personal consciousness. What do you choose in life? What are your heart's desires? Those desires are Spirit, the Love and Law vibrations as one, pressing upon you to express Itself in the phenomenal world. Move in mind to the great reservoir of Intelligent Substance, and feel the flow of creative energy taking place through you. Now reach in mind to the Truth of your Being, the Knowing Mind Who sees you abundantly rich, whole, and well, totally successful in all that you do, and loved and loving in ideal relationships. Capture that Vision, be in the flow, and let it come to pass.

Contemplations

God is fully manifest as all aspects of my being. God is my individual being, my reality. All that God is, I AM. All that God has is mine. I am totally complete.

Within my Divine Mind is the perfect idea of everything I could possibly need, want, or desire in this world. I now look through Spirit's eyes and see the Holy Vision. Guidance and protection are overshadowing me at every moment. I am blessed with ideal relationships, true place success, the perfect body, financial plenty, and every form and experience that would contribute to blissful living. All that I could ever seek, I have.

As I focus my mind on the Truth of my being, the Holy Vision, all that is within my consciousness is eternally and easily being extended, expressed, and made manifest in the phenomenal world without any effort on my part. Forms of utter delight are continually being revealed. Experiences of great joy are constantly pouring through my Self-awareness to be lived by me in pleasure and jubilation.

I dedicate my life to the Spirit of God I AM. I relax. I contemplate. I listen. I watch. The law of harmony is now ruling my world.

CHAPTER FOUR

The Divine Design

Our personal consciousness once knew itself to be God in expression, and even after the fall-into-unknowing, an awareness, understanding, and knowledge of our divine nature remained. It's a Light in our energy field that has never gone out. Although surrounded and imprisoned by sense consciousness, this Splendor has always been the shining brilliance of the Living Truth within.

This Truth is the manifest Christ, the Universal I AM of the Fourth Dimension in a vibration of I AM on Earth, our Divine Identity expressed on the plane of the third dimension. And Jesus said, *"You shall know the truth, and the truth shall make you free"* (John 8:32).

As the awareness of our spiritual nature dimmed, our Divine Consciousness, the Supreme I AM, extended a ray of

Light into our feeling nature to maintain the Divine Identity. This Light from above also included the Divine Design, given to us to open all doors for joyous fulfillment on the physical plane.

Mystics have said that the Divine Design is emerald green in color and diamond shaped, or a square tilted to appear as a diamond, surrounded by the Christ-Truth as a golden light. The reason for this four-square design is that it incorporates the four aspects considered paramount for third-dimensional living: abundance, physical wholeness, creative self-expression, and loving relationships. It's the four-square of life, fully present now, developed and eternally preserved by spiritual forces. These are the Archetypes that serve as Living Energies to help us on our journey through life. We'll discuss those aspects of Spirit in the next chapter—for now, let's focus on the Divine Design.

Each of the four sides or angles of the diamond represents a specific pattern or blueprint for the manifestation of energy into form and experience:

1. The Abundance Pattern is a splendid collection of power circuits for the radiation, manifestation, attraction, and expansion of financial supply, including the channels through which the supply will reach us and the plan for our continued financial support.

2. The Pattern for Physical Wholeness embodies the lines of force to heal, restore, revitalize, strengthen, nourish, and reinvigorate our body, and to maintain it in a state of excellent health.

3. The Success Pattern is the creative force of grand achievement, the spirit of accomplishment, the energy of divine aspiration to fill our highest destiny. It's creative self-expression, ever illuminated by the higher vision.

4. The Relationship Pattern is filled with convergence points for meeting the right person, for attracting only loving and harmonious people into our lives, for healing all individual conflicts of the past and present, for making the right decisions regarding interaction with others, and for choosing the right mate.

As I stated earlier, surrounding the four-sided diamond is the energy of I AM, the manifest Christ, our true Identity fully expressed in the realm of the third dimension. This is the Truth that says, *"I AM ABUNDANCE, I AM WHOLE AND PERFECT, I AM SUCCESS, I AM LOVED AND LOVING. I AM COMPLETE."*

Can we understand the importance of this? It means that our Divine Identity and the Truth of our abundance, wholeness, success, and loving relationships have been extended as a ray of light from the *Knower* to the *Doer,* from the Fourth Dimension to the third, from Divine Consciousness to Creative Mind, the law side of Spirit.

These lines of force and vibrations of energy are firmly in place, but unless we know and accept these Gifts, the creative power of manifestation will flow through a consciousness of scarcity, imperfection, futility, conflict, or the masks that bind us. It's like slides in a projector: The slides for a wonderfully fulfilling life are there, but where are we directing the light?

The river of substance, the light, is always flowing. When we're consciously aware of the Divine Design in our hearts, the river follows that awareness. It becomes the river of wealth, the river of health, the river of success, the river of right relations. The river is the all-inclusive supply—why divert it into fearful, limiting thoughtforms? With the Divine Design, every need has been met, every problem solved, yet we pray for relief from a situation or condition, thus denying our Truth of Being.

When a fearful thought about money comes to mind, fasten your gaze on the pattern of abundance. Become consciously aware of it. See and feel the light shining through it as the river of wealth, moving out into the phenomenal world to appear as an all-sufficiency of funds. Remember that unlimited abundance is a natural part of life on the third-dimensional plane. We are the Allness of God in unique expression, and in the individualizing process, nothing was left out. Right at this moment, regardless of seeming circumstances, the lavish wealth of the universe is within us, flowing out into visibility through our conscious awareness of its instant availability.

In *Angel Energy,* I wrote:

> Whenever we experience a shortage of money, it means that we are registering a sense of *want*—a feeling of incompletion—rather than a realization of *have.* How strange this is. We have been given everything, and the kingdom within is bulging with awesome abundance, yet we see scarcity, which is a direct denial of our true nature. No wonder that Emerson said that "wealth is moral . . . the only sin is limitation."[1]

When a concern about the body pops up, focus your attention on the paradigm of physical wholeness. Our body is flawless and unimpaired at every moment of our journey on the third-dimensional plane, for there is nothing but perfection throughout the infinite universe:

> This is the truth of our being, and if our physical system seems to say otherwise, it is because we are believing a lie. . . . Is the physical body real? Yes, because it is energy in configuration appearing as a body. Is it perfect? Yes, as the energy of the spiritual body manifesting as form—but it is made imperfect in our experience to the degree of

imperfection held in consciousness. As consciousness real-
izes its perfect wholeness as the Mind of God in expression,
so will the body, because the body is subjective to mind.[2]

Is there futility in your work or career plan? Connect with
the success pattern. And remember that success is the natural
order of the universe, wholly ordained by God as a force for
good to replace the effects of this world with divine Reality.
Success is based on the ideal *to do, to be*—that which you pas-
sionately *choose* to achieve and accomplish. What is your
image of true success? That which you can conceive in mind
as the ideal goal in life, your master intention, must already
be a part of your consciousness; otherwise, you could not conceive of it as a possible reality.

If you're experiencing discord with another person, see the
light shining through the love pattern. Now you're setting up
the vibration to attract and harmonize your relationships,
and to loosen those that don't belong in your life. This pattern
represents the energy of goodwill and cooperation for the
benefit of the planetary family, where you're at peace with all
the world, and all the world is at peace with you.

And if you find yourself wearing any of the masks that hold
you in bondage as a false persona, remember that you are the
I AM of God, the manifest Christ on Earth, and see everyone
else with that same Divine Identity. Let your I AM be the I AM
That I AM, and think and speak from that Holy Vibration. That
is where the power is.

See the full four-sided diamond as the perfect pattern for
ideal living, and see the rushing waters of life pouring through
it. Remember, energy follows thought.

ONE NIGHT WHEN I COULDN'T FALL ASLEEP, I contemplated the
Divine Design, the emerald-green diamond in my heart. To my
surprise, it began to glow and grow, expanding in all its

brilliance until it was larger than my physical body. In my imagination, I got out of bed and stepped into the pulsating fire of the diamond—and it literally took my breath away. It was as though I'd moved into another dimension, a realm of serenity, love, and harmony. While in this state of completion, I fell sound asleep. And the dreams began—experiences of great joy with friends, sharings of abundance, awesome beauty, and feelings of total fulfillment. In the days that followed, the tone, pitch, and flavor of the dreams manifested themselves in the phenomenal world as marvelous things happening. The inner had become the outer.

This showed me that the Divine Design is *alive*. It's composed of Living Energies, and the more we're aware of it, the greater the activation of those energies in our lives.

Contemplations

I acknowledge that Spirit has already provided for everything I could possibly desire in life. I have the Divine Design. I feel it anchored in my heart.

That which I was seeking is fully expressed within me. Therefore, I have no unfulfilled desires. All is complete.

This total fulfillment is etched permanently in my heart. I see it as four patterns of light, the sacred diamond blazing in consciousness with the I AM Truth encompassing it.

I see the great river of life flowing through my Divine Design. I feel its incredible rushing force.

Now I see the green diamond growing, expanding into a holy structure, beckoning me. Without hesitation,

I step into it and feel the fire electric. All false beliefs and error patterns are being burned away.

I am clear and clean, and the river of wealth, wholeness, success, and loving relations is pouring through me. It is done.

This dynamic energy is now moving to be in the outer what it is in the inner. I am a Complete Being.

CHAPTER FIVE

The Master Builders

T he Archetypes, also referred to as "the angels within,"
aren't only the builders and maintainers of the Divine
Design based on the Thoughtform of Spirit, but they also
strengthen and condition consciousness. They emanate from
Divine Mind, much like shining rays from the sun. They represent particular energy vibrations, manifesting agents of
Spirit to bring our lives up to the divine standard. They're a
unified field, clusters of living intelligence and power in an
interconnecting mass of energy, which exist just beyond the
conscious level of mind.

Remember that the manifest Christ represents the Truth
of your Identity on the personal level, and uses the Living
Energies as its agents in freeing you from ego projections
of a false identity. This Holy Self in a three-dimensional

vibration maintains the Divine Identity, your Truth. And when you identify with this Truth—in concert with the angels within—the vibration of your entire energy field changes. It becomes more transparent for the activity of Spirit.

The four Master Builders and Maintainers of the Divine Design are:

1. The Angel of Abundance. In Ageless Wisdom, she's known as the *Venus Archetype*. She partakes of the planetary energy of Venus, and her symbolic representation (tarot) is The High Priestess. Her work is to develop the perfect pattern of abundance, ensuring an all-sufficiency of financial plenty at all times. Her leadership role in the Divine Design (the top right angle) is important because a sense of scarcity, loss, and limitation has a direct influence on health, creative success, and relationships. It's also said that we cannot have peace in this world without prosperity.

2. The Angel of Truth and Enlightenment. This Aspect of Spirit (the bottom right angle of the diamond) was known by the Egyptians as the archetype *Ra,* a being of the sun representing the power that resurrects the soul. To the Greeks, he was known as *Apollo,* the god of the sun and light. In the ancient tarot, the card signifying this angel is the Sun, the same identification as in esoteric astrology. His primary activity is to overshadow the healing pattern, ensuring the right vibration in the physical body to maintain health and wholeness.

3. The Angel of Success. The Success Archetype was called *Kronos* in some early Mystery Schools, a being who destroyed seeming limitations of time in the third-dimensional world to reveal the divine Reality in the Now moment. In other sacred academies, this Causal Power was called *Saturn*, the bringer of gifts and the deliverer of rewards. The legend of Santa Claus came directly from the Saturn teachings in the old schools. In the tarot, this power is symbolized by the World, a card signifying the final and successful completion of any matter. It is fulfillment, the sum total of creation, and represents the pattern of true-place success (bottom left angle) in the Divine Design.

4. The Angel of Loving Relationships. In the upper left angle is *Anubis*—associated with the sun in the Egyptian schools as a symbol of enlightenment and immortality. This Angel spreads its wings, so to speak, over the pattern of right relations and helps us make the correct choice in all personal relationships. In the tarot, this energy form is symbolized by the Lovers, representing the responsibility for making right choices. The symbolism illustrates duality unified, the male and female complementing each other.

The 22 Angels were the original Archetypes or patterns of the universe. They're the divine ideas of God from which all things came forth. From a personal sense, Spirit has considered every feeling, emotion, mind-set, problem, situation, and experience, and has given us the way out, the solution, the answer.

While the 4 Archetypes noted above represent the guardians of the four-square Divine Design, the other 18 play a vital role in consciousness. They are, as follows:

5. The Angel of Unconditional Love and Freedom teaches harmlessness and functions as the fountain for the outpouring of Universal Love, and assists in the realization of your divinity and the divinity of others. *Archetype:* Tao, Krishna, Master of Heaven. *Planetary Energy:* Uranus. *Symbolic (Tarot):* The Fool.

6. The Angel of Illusion and Reality helps you separate false from true in life through the energy of creative intelligence. It's the illuminating principle that releases the mind from bondage and enables you to be aware of the divine plan. *Archetype:* Hermes, Mercury. *Planetary Energy:* Mercury. *Symbolic (Tarot):* The Magician.

7. The Angel of Creative Wisdom helps you solve problems quickly, imparts spiritual wisdom, ensures that judgment is clear and correct, and stimulates instinctive action. *Archetype:* Isis. *Planetary Energy:* Moon. *Symbolic (Tarot):* The High Priestess.

8. The Angel of Power and Authority provides great energy and determination, and strong decisiveness with reliance on the will of God in every situation. *Archetype:* Osiris, Hercules. *Planetary Energy:* Aries. *Symbolic (Tarot):* The Emperor.

9. The Angel of Spiritual Understanding lifts the vibration of consciousness to the level of spiritual perception. It is the energy of open-mindedness, enabling the aspirant to learn deep esoteric truths. *Archetype:* The Grand Master. *Planetary Energy:* Taurus. *Symbolic (Tarot):* The High Priest.

10. The Angel of Victory and Triumph is the archetype of the conqueror, helps you meet your objective with determination, and stimulates tenacity and resolution. *Archetype:* Serapis. *Planetary Energy:* Cancer. *Symbolic (Tarot):* The Chariot.

11. The Angel of Order and Harmony is the peace vibration in consciousness, which helps you maintain balance and fairness in all situations and inspires you to live with integrity. *Archetype:* Athena, Minerva. *Planetary Energy:* Libra. *Symbolic (Tarot):* Justice.

12. The Angel of Discernment works best in moments of solitude to train your mind to be prudent and judicious; it also helps you take actions based on proper discernment. *Archetype:* Adonis. *Planetary Energy:* Virgo. *Symbolic (Tarot):* The Hermit.

13. The Angel of Cycles and Solutions provides the ability to accept change and move into expansive cycles with the attitude that nothing but absolute good is taking place. Also called the *Energy of Miracles. Archetype:* Zeus, Jupiter. *Planetary Energy:* Jupiter. *Symbolic (Tarot):* The Wheel of Fortune.

14. The Angel of Spiritual Strength and Will helps you have the mental will, emotional determination, and physical fortitude to follow the spiritual path regardless of worldly temptations. *Archetype:* Daughter of the Flaming Sword. *Planetary Energy:* Leo. *Symbolic (Tarot):* Strength.

15. The Angel of Renunciation and Regeneration provides the energy of surrender, showing you the ease and beauty of "having nothing in order to possess everything." *Archetype:* Poseidon, Neptune. *Planetary Energy:* Neptune. *Symbolic (Tarot):* The Hanged Man.

16. The Angel of Death and Rebirth is called the *Energy of Metamorphosis.* This archetype helps you cross out the ego and realize your identity as a spiritual being. *Archetype:* Thanatos, Death. *Planetary Energy:* Scorpio. *Symbolic (Tarot):* Death.

17. The Angel of Patience and Acceptance provides the energy that enables you to trust the divine process with total acceptance of "come what may," living day-to-day with calm equanimity. *Archetype:* Iris, Queen of Heaven. *Planetary Energy:* Sagittarius. *Symbolic (Tarot):* Temperance.

18. The Angel of Materiality and Temptation helps you stay grounded until you're spiritually ready to awaken into Fourth-Dimensional consciousness, while protecting you from going too far with a preoccupation with effects. *Archetype:* Janus. *Planetary Energy:* Capricorn. *Symbolic (Tarot):* Old Pan.

19. The Angel of Courage and Perseverance provides the energy of steadfastness, the courage to live only the Truth of Being and to persevere in that consciousness—regardless of what's going on around you. *Archetype:* Aries, Mars. *Planetary Energy:* Mars. *Symbolic (Tarot):* The Tower.

20. The Angel of Service and Synthesis motivates you to greater service in the world and helps you understand why service is a primary requisite for achieving mastery. *Archetype:* Ganymede. *Planetary Energy:* Aquarius. *Symbolic (Tarot):* The Star.

21. The Angel of Imagination and Liberation teaches you to image abstractly and see with the inner eye, strengthening the spiritual vision that enables you to see the Truth of the finished Kingdom—a higher vision of Reality that can be fully manifested on the third-dimensional plane. *Archetype:* Artemis, Diana. *Planetary Energy:* Pisces. *Symbolic (Tarot):* The Moon.

22. The Angel of the Creative Word releases energy to move consciousness above miscreations into the realm of Cause, where the spoken word can be used to correct situations and settle matters for the good of all. *Archetype:* Hades, Pluto, Phoenix. *Planetary Energy:* Pluto. *Symbolic (Tarot):* The Judgment.

It's a fascinating and delightful experience to work with the angels. They'll help you break the grip of ego and rise into a new frequency of consciousness. To meet an angel, first consent to the truth that these whirlpools of power exist within you. Then go into meditation and contemplate these energies of Spirit as ministering angels, or hands of God, which you're given on your journey through life. Next, ask your Inner Guide to come forth and take you to meet the one of your choice. Relax . . . let your imaging faculty come into play, and feel yourself being guided into the inner planes. A light will appear and begin to take shape as a man, a woman, or a symbolic form to correspond to your tone of consciousness. At that point, let the dialogue begin.

As a starting point, you might ask the appropriate angel to tell you why you're experiencing less-than-desirable conditions in finances, health, career, or relationships. In one of my first contacts with the Angel of Abundance, she said: "When you finally moved into your true place, which was a life of spiritual communications, you could not fully reconcile the idea that spiritual work justified abundance. Because you are in spiritual work, the value of money in your mind is lessened even more through a false belief that says spirituality and abundance are irreconcilable. Abundance is yours, regardless of the work you do, if you do not equate what you do with making money. Do what you love to do most and equate the money in your life with the endless stream of energy flowing from the source."

In a later conversation, she told me, "Lasting material riches must come forth from inner spiritual riches. There is no other way." This causal power of prosperity also reminded me that money is energy, and that it's drawn particularly to those who appreciate beauty, quality, order, and harmony. The angel explained: "This energy is of royal origin, born of love and ripened in the kingdom of grace and beauty, and is attracted to an individual who represents a close affinity with that vibration. There are exceptions, but in the long term, one who is slovenly repels the energy, while a loving and noble character evokes it. A person's bearing, especially when warmed with deep unconditional love and a spirit of goodwill, is a crucial attribute in the attraction of financial supply."

The Angel of Success was also very helpful to me. He said, "I am moldable, impressionable, for I am subjective to you. I become your vibration, and I remove everything unlike your vibration in your world. I follow the orders of your consciousness. If there is vacillation, as in your consciousness of success, I will vacillate between seeming triumphs and disappointments." I soon learned that a success vibration in mind and heart will work wonders in the phenomenal world.

The angels will work with us in many different ways. Following are some other examples.

When Frank in Georgia discovered the Angel of Success, he immediately thought of quitting his job and forming his own company for greater freedom and opportunity. He wrote:

> I had even written my letter of resignation, but before I could submit it, I heard, "Wait. Explore the possibilities here. Ask about the planned expansion and your role in the new organization."
>
> I went to my boss the next morning and said that "my intuition tells me that something is going on behind the scenes, and I'd like to know how it's going

to affect me." He looked surprised and said that my gut feeling was right on—that a merger with another firm was in the works, that it was all very confidential now, but that I was being looked at to head up one of the new divisions.

That was six months ago. Now I've got my cake and I'm eating it, too, because it's like running my own company but with all the perks of a long-established organization. And I've never been happier with my work. I owe the Angel of Success a debt of gratitude.

Elizabeth in Philadelphia visited the Angel of Truth and Enlightenment about her arthritis:

I asked him to shine through me and eliminate everything in my objective awareness that denied my perfection. I held myself in the light of the Sun [Archetype] and felt the divine rays shining through me. I repeated this process several times during the day, and recorded in my journal the changes that were taking place in consciousness. After three days, the pain went away and has not returned.

Allen in Boston wrote:

I hadn't felt really good for a long time . . . had tests by the doctors but they couldn't find anything. Your talk about inspiration did motivate me to try it, but it didn't work—that is, until I met with the Angel of Courage and Perseverance. He's been working with me to show me that I do have something to look forward to in life, and as the inspiration grows, the tiredness goes.

Jupiter, the Angel of Cycles and Solutions, once appeared before my wife, Jan, in Roman clothes with a wreath on his head, saying, "Nero fiddled while Rome was burning. As for you, I can only expand what you give me to expand." He then changed his appearance and became the head and upper body of a centaur, which symbolizes aspiration and ambition. Jan felt that he was telling her to stop frittering away time, that she was ignoring an important opportunity during this period to examine and contemplate certain personal and business activities that would be highlighted in the next upward spiral. Finally, he said, "Focus your thoughts on what you really want in life."

As you work toward life-changing experiences, I suggest that you spend time with the Jupiter Archetype. In the Mystery Schools, he was known as the *Causal Power of Expansion* and *the Angel of Miracles.* Unless blocked by ego projections of thoughts, such as, *This is too good to be true, This good can't last,* or *I just know something bad is going to happen,* this angel will help you stay firmly on the path, regardless of what's going on in your world. In this regard, you might remember . . .

The Angel of Cycles and Solutions is my holy helper, my guide on the pathway to illumination. In my oneness with the Spirit of God I AM, I see change as the natural order of things, as the breathing in and breathing out in the divine process of manifestation. Without hesitation, I fully accept change in my life, knowing that only my highest good is expressed in every upward cycle.

Here's a checklist that may be helpful to you in working with the other angels.

If You're Experiencing	See the Angel of
Apathy	Success
Accidents	Discernment, Order and Harmony
Anger	Order and Harmony, Courage and Perseverance
Confusion	Illusion and Reality, Patience and Acceptance
Danger	Courage and Perseverance
Defeat	Spiritual Strength and Will, Victory and Triumph
Depression	Spiritual Strength and Will
Domestic problems	Abundance, Loving Relationships
Failure	Success, Victory and Triumph
Fear	Imagination and Liberation, Illusion and Reality, Renunciation and Regeneration, Service and Synthesis, Unconditional Love and Freedom
Guilt	Creative Word, Illusion and Reality, Loving Relationships
Lack	Abundance
Legal problems	Creative Word
Physical problems	Truth and Enlightenment
Relationship problems	Loving Relationships, Order and Harmony

Self-doubt	Service and Synthesis, Success
Sexual problems	Abundance, Loving Relationships
Victim consciousness	Power and Authority, Renunciation and Regeneration

Think now, God is all you are. Your Divine Constitution includes the one Mind in different modes of expression as the *Knower, Chooser,* and *Doer.* And surrounding the *Chooser* aspect are 22 whirlpools of Living Energy that condition and determine all outer expression. But there's more. We've also been given the Divine Design to ensure that we live a complete life on this plane of existence, with abundant supply, magnificent health, creative self-expression, and right relations. And we have the manifest I AM Identity that brings omnipotence to our thoughts and words.

Isn't it time to realize our inheritance and live in a literal Heaven on Earth?

Yes!

CHAPTER SIX
Climbing Jacob's Ladder

Jacob represents the mind of understanding, our mental faculty focused on living life to the fullest—spiritually, mentally, emotionally, and physically. *Ladder* signifies our step-by-step realizations of Truth, beginning with the knowledge that Spirit withholds nothing from us, that the most complete life in all its aspects is our divine birthright.

Why are we not living the ideal life? Because of certain attitudes we're entertaining in mind and heart—attitudes that tell us that we aren't deserving of abundance and perfect harmony in relationships, that we aren't good enough to experience creative success, and that wholeness of body isn't our lot in life. Or we blame everything on other people, conditions, situations, and circumstances.

As we place our foot on the first rung of the ladder, we should have the intention to change our minds and see ourselves—and life—differently. And we do this first by loving, approving, and embracing the totality of ourselves. Look at yourself: What is it that you don't like? Pause for a moment and think about this. Now consider the people in your life, from the center core of family on out to friends, acquaintances, co-workers, and so on. What is it that you don't like about them? Pause for reflection. Now look at your life in all its aspects. See yourself living on planet Earth, in a particular location, doing what you do in interaction with others. What is it that you don't like about your life? Look closely and be honest in your response, then think on these thoughts:

I choose to forgive myself and everyone else in this world. I choose to forgive all negative aspects of my life as I perceive them. If there is anyone or anything I feel I cannot forgive, I forgive my unforgiveness and ask my Holy Self to forgive through me. I choose to be free of any and all resentment.

Now begin to love yourself more and see only peace in this world.

TO *FORGIVE* MEANS TO CEASE FEELING ILL WILL toward anyone, but in truth there's really nothing to forgive. You've never done anything wrong, no one has ever done anything to you, and life is only what you've made up—what you've created. Every decision you've ever made in life was simply a choice, and through those choices, your life has taken many twists and turns. But none of them were right or wrong—it's just where you were in consciousness. So there's nothing to forgive yourself for. And rather than going back and rehashing the past and wishing you'd done things differently, just love the mind-set that made the choice and get on with life. Pause and do this now. By loving what you consider your mistakes, you change the energy pattern on the unconscious level from regret to acceptance of where you were at the time. Now look at the people in your life, and know that it's your consciousness in the projection mode that's attracting or repelling them. No one has done, or is doing, anything to you. The people in your life are all neutral, but will play out an experience for you in direct accordance with the tone and pitch *you're* playing in consciousness. They're simply showing you what you're projecting on them, so there's nothing to forgive them for. The secret in dissolving this energy is to love those who are playing a role on your stage of life for playing their parts perfectly—parts that you've scripted on both the conscious and unconscious levels. Smile and nod at them now in appreciation.

Change the vision in your mind now to the spectrum of your entire life—your physical system, your finances, your creative activities, and your relationships. You've been scripting every detail in your creative imagination—again, consciously or unconsciously. *You* have the power to be well or sick, or rich or poor; to succeed or fail; and to live in harmony or conflict. Instead of trying to forgive yourself for what you may consider to be an improper use of that power, begin to love the part of yourself that attracted illness, scarcity, failure, and discord. Yes, they're all worthy of love.

When we love those causal thoughtforms and unconscious beliefs, their energy changes and a healing soon takes place. Do this now. Love the part of you that accepted a malady in the body. Love that reactive emotion that believed in scarcity. Love the state of mind that has experienced failure. Love that misguided energy that attracted less-than-perfect harmony in relationships. Love, approve, and embrace the *totality* of you, and let the healing take place.

Now Look at Your Greatest Fear

Bring it to the surface of mind. Ageless Wisdom tells us that fear is only the product of ignorance, not wrong thinking. And what's the opposite of ignorance? *Understanding.* Do you fear that you won't have enough money later in life? Move from ignorance to understanding by contemplating your Divine Design, and know that you're the treasure house of the universe, with an all-inclusive supply—the very creative energy of money. "What you see you shall become," said Jesus. What are you seeing? What are you feeling? Riches in mind and heart must by law come forth as riches in manifestation. To fear not having enough equates with lack, and lack always attracts more lack.

Do you fear disease and illness? What we fear will come upon us, and that's working out of ignorance. The truth is, the body cannot be sick—it only reflects. Except for ailments relating to the nervous system, which originate in the mental realm, all physical maladies begin in the emotional system— and emotions are the seat of fear. Let's move from ignorance to understanding by knowing that we have a choice. Spirit sees us as perfect and so we are. Let's choose that vision and live life fully.

As I was writing this chapter, a friend in Georgia sent me an e-mail that ties in nicely with this subject. He wrote:

I was 17 before my family had a refrigerator to store food in, and we cooked food that had been set out for two or three days at a time, yet now we're told that we must not let food set out more than two or three hours or we're sure to be poisoned. We butchered pigs in early winter, let uncooked sausage sit in open pans for weeks, and cooked everything in continuously recycled pig fat, yet no one ever got sick. And in spite of a very unhealthy diet of lots of white flour, grease, and sugar, none of my people ever spent time in a nursing home—they all lived to old age. Many of the folks I spent lots of time with raised sheep, common carriers of anthrax, but no one got sick, let alone died from it. You would be shocked if I told you some of the stuff that was everyday life for us as well as our neighbors, but the result is I will outlive all but the youngest because my immune system has had a chance to come up with a defense for almost every ailment known to man.

My Georgia friend probably knows that in Divine Mind, there's no idea or consciousness of germs, viruses, toxins, bacteria, high blood pressure, high cholesterol, or other such "causes." Therefore, they don't exist in the *real* sense. We made them up, and for those who have accepted them, they appear to be real.

Do you fear death? As my wife, Jan, knows full well from her journey beyond the veil, death does not exist. Life just springs from one plane to another when it's time to drop the body.

I had a mind-image experience that proved this to me. Jan and I were driving to town and saw a deer lying by the side of the road. In my mind, I saw the whole scenario in a split second: A truck struck the deer and threw it up in the air, but even before it landed in the ditch, I saw it suddenly come forth out of its fleshly body and scamper into the woods, moving through the veil in a flash of light and continuing to run with joy in the Heavenly fields beyond. *There is no death.*

Do you have a fear regarding relationships? Let it go. Relax. Let those relationships end that should be ended. Let those relationships where you should be more detached move in that direction. Let those relationships that should be brought into a closer bond do so. And if you seek a love-mate relationship, don't fear you won't have one. He or she is already there, waiting for you to dissolve your fear.

In the past year, we've heard comments about other fears—of flying, of prowlers, of road rage, of the government's unrestricted powers. Here's an exercise that will help you move beyond such fears:

Sit in a comfortable chair and completely relax. Think about the fear, then reverse the process. Move in mind to the opposite effect—that is, place your attention on what you want, rather than what you don't want.

Let's take the fear of flying as an example. You're going to take a flight in your imagination, making it a subjective experience.

Mentally project yourself as you easily board the plane. See the happy smiles and hear the greetings of the flight attendants. Find your seat with friendly companions all around you. You are totally relaxed, and there is a feeling of joyous expectation of a perfect flight, of arriving at your destination on time and with ease. You hear the mighty engines start up, feel the plane being pulled from the gate, its forward thrust as it moves into position for takeoff, and then the race down the runway. You look out the window at the beauty below as the plane banks and moves into its flight pattern. It is a fun ride with interesting people, and the pleasure continues on your journey. You chat with someone, read, or take a nap. Now hear the captain on the intercom: "Folks, we'll be landing soon," followed by a delightful weather report. Then you come in for a smooth landing and arrive at the gate— a most pleasant experience.

This is not idle daydreaming, for what you experience in your imagination will be developed on the subjective level of mind, and fears relating to flying will be dissolved. That's the law of the *Doer*. It cannot fail.

More on What's Blocking Our Good

We've taken several steps up Jacob's Ladder, and we'll continue with greater understanding in the chapters that follow. But let's pause for a moment and focus more closely on the blocks that may be held below the conscious level of mind.

At one point in my life, I asked my Spirit to show me any barriers that may be screening out my good. Here is the answer I received: "If you think there are impediments, there are. That's your judgment, which will be upheld by law. Blocks are only attitudes. The hindrances are what you perceive to be real, but are nothing but beliefs."

I pondered this for a moment and realized that there are some strange beliefs within the human family: the belief that your work, what you do, may not be approved by someone, which then repels others from the fruits of that work; the belief that you're not worthy, not deserving, of abundance, which limits the flow; the belief that you do not have enough of (whatever), which the law then proves that you don't; the belief that you're not appreciated, thus moving you into loneliness and passivity; the belief that you've been wronged, which attracts more similar situations; the belief that you've *done* something wrong, which puts out a silent call for punishment. I'm sure you can add to the list.

Then I asked, "What's the answer?"

I was told the following: "All one has to do is see things differently. Look at the cup that needs to be filled, and ask why it is not. The present belief will come to mind. Now simply correct that belief. Reverse the thinking, and see what you wish to see. There are no troubling situations. The only problem is how you perceive it. Rely not on the past for your perceptions; see only the truth of the now with vision divine. There are no limitations in life. There never have been."

WITH THESE REMINDERS, let's change our mind, our attitude, about every activity of life in this world. Let's see what we want to see with expanded and uplifted vision, and refuse to think that there's anything in Heaven or Earth that could possibly hold back our good . . . and that includes any old false beliefs.

When we reverse our attitudes about life, and accept all that's already good, true, and beautiful, we move into the *have* consciousness. That's when it will be proved to us that *nothing is too good to be true.*

CHAPTER SEVEN
You Are the Law Unto Your World

The great metaphysician Emmet Fox tells us that Principle, or Law, is the least understood of the main aspects of God. In his book *Alter Your Life*, he writes: "God is the Principle (Law) of perfect harmony and God does not change, so perfect harmony is the nature of his creation. . . . Scientific prayer does not try to change the Law. It does not try to bring about exceptions in our favor. It does not ask God to change the laws of nature for our temporary convenience, but it tunes us in, so to speak, with Divine Principle, and then we find things coming right."[1]

Charles Fillmore, in the *Metaphysical Bible Dictionary*, writes: "The law of God is the orderly working out of the principle of Being, or the divine ideals, into expression and manifestation throughout creation."[2] And Ernest Holmes, in

The Science of Mind, says that when we use the Law, it becomes *our* law. "The possibilities of the Law are infinite," he writes, "and our possibilities of using It are limitless."[3]

It is said that the Law is impersonal, yet I believe that we must become personal to It. Ageless Wisdom is emphatic in stating that the reason we don't enjoy the fullness of abundant life is because we don't work (personally identify) with the creative feminine medium, the *Doer,* the law of all manifestation.

To me, the Law is a Presence, a Creative Mind possessing the absolute certainties of the Cosmic Mandates. Taking it one step at a time, let's look at the whole process of Law as it reveals that which is good, true, and beautiful in our lives.

1. Recognize the Divine Feminine within as the Law, Force, and Power of all manifest form and experience. This aspect of the Whole Spirit known as the Divine Mother is the source and cause of all visible effects. She is creative energy, substance, light, the agent of Divine Will. She is universal and individual, eternally flowing through the state of consciousness that we're holding before Her. However, through our use of free will, we're able to break her laws, be arrested (seized in consciousness), and through the self-pronouncement of guilt, go through a punishment stage appropriate for the offense. But now we're going to walk the path rightly, take control of our lives, and live as the Masters of our Destiny.

Quoting Emmet Fox again:

> . . . the Law gives you power to bring any condition into your life that is not harmful. The law gives you power to overcome your own weaknesses and faults of character, no matter how often you may have failed in the past or how tenacious they may have seemed to be. The Law gives you power to attain prosperity and position without infringing the rights and opportunities of anyone else in the world.

The Law gives you Independence so that you can build your own life in your own way, in accordance with your own ideas and ideals; and plan out your future along the lines that you yourself desire.[4]

2. The Law's Commandments: *"You must be . . . "* are absolute Cosmic Pronouncements of Truth.
In *Angel Energy*, I wrote:

> Spiritual Law is the way the universe works. It is energy in action according to a predetermined objective, as in the Law of Wholeness, the Law of Abundance, the Law of Love. It is the Power of God in operation as *Cause*, as *Principle*, as *Truth*. It is the sum total of the Omniscience Energy of the universe saying, "This is the way it is, and nothing can change my mind. You are forever whole and flawless, abundantly supplied with every good thing, experiencing love in every encounter, enjoying success and fulfillment in every activity of life, and remaining eternally in a state of gladness, joy, and contentment."
>
> But when we don't know the Law, or are not consciously aware of the way things really are, we make up our own laws, and then we have to live with them until they are repealed through an understanding that these self-imposed ordinances are in violation of our own inner Supreme Court.
>
> Isn't it time to get out of the law-making business and rely only on the Constitution of Being, the Original Statutes of God?[5]

The basic idea in this second step is that in the workings of the Law, there are Divine Imperatives, Commandments that say, in effect, that's the way it is regardless of your beliefs, arguments, or resistance. You need only to agree and accept. Nothing else is necessary.

To explain further, look at wealth, abundance, prosperity, and riches from the standpoint of the material plane. This state of affairs is a mandate, an order, an edict, a decree: "You *must*, by law, be rich." There's no way around it from the divine view because the Divine Design is in place, the Creative Principle has absolutely no limitations, and never measures out just a few riches into manifestation. Her energy-in-expression flows unending, in full force with equal and total distribution for all. Emerson knew this when he wrote: "Man is born to be rich." Women, too, I might add.

In *Scientific Christian Mental Practice*, Emma Curtis Hopkins writes:

> Everybody, early, tries to cover up the main purpose of his life. He tells all kinds of stories to himself and others about what he is seeking. Often he tells that all he asks is just enough to feed and clothe and house his family. Let him tell the honest Truth—that he seeks for unlimited bounty. Nothing can possibly satisfy anybody short of unlimited supply. God is the idea of unlimited supply which men keep covered so deeply within their minds. If you name your Good, do not fail to say: "My Good is my unlimited support, my unfailing support." The Good will soon bring you marvelous support. New provisions will be made for you. There is no limit to the bounty of Truth. The substance of Truth is shown by the happy prosperity which can come to you, and is sure to come, when you speak Truth.[6]

Why is abundance "written on the heart" as a law? Why is money a divine idea and a spiritual asset? Because Infinite Wisdom knows that there's a need on the physical plane for a medium of exchange, an instrument of goodwill. Without the proper funds to live a life of all-sufficiency, consciousness depresses, fear enters, and we resort to manipulating, begging, borrowing, or stealing. Not helpful activities in the reawakening process of realizing Who and What we are. Therefore, we're provided with all that we could possibly need or want in a particular lifetime.

The Law has already given us a lavish abundance, which is appearing as money. "Where is it?" you might ask. "It certainly isn't in my bank account." The money may not be in your bank account yet, but it's certainly out there in manifest form, touched by Creative Mind with your coded imprint. And there's more than you could possibly need in this incarnation, once you understand the Law.

I realize that not everyone wants to be *really* rich. They don't want the responsibilities, the so-called pressures of wealth. So they find what they consider the appropriate level of comfort/contentment in the mental-emotional nature, and perhaps unconsciously turn the supply valve to off. Nothing wrong with that—we're our own experience based on the decisions we make in life.

The perfection of the physical body follows the same rule of Law: "You *must*, by Law, be perfect—*now.*" We've been given the perfect pattern for physical wholeness, and by law we cannot be sick or diseased. In Divine Mind, there's only perfection. Within Consciousness is the idea of the perfect body, and this Ideal Pattern is constantly seeking to renew the body after Itself.

Let's lift up our vision and see as God sees—a radiantly healthy body filled with peace and joy. As we see ourselves doing everything we want to do—energetically, enthusiastically, and easily—there's a definite shift in our energy fields because *energy follows thought*. We visualize our body as a dynamic vehicle for every physical expression that we enjoy doing, and see ourselves demonstrating a wonderful sense of well-being. Let's be the Law of Perfection unto our body.

Look now at success, which is indeed a commandment: "You *must*, by Law, be successful." What does that mean? It means that we're here on the physical plane to make this a better world through the creative activity of service—of accomplishment and achievement. And if we don't, we'll move into that state called "creeping inertia"—without inspiration or zest for life. That's against the law.

When we work with this Law, rather than against it, we're shown our True Place and given the opportunities to use our talents to the fullest—including those we haven't as yet recognized. And we'll find decisions being made for us by Creative Mind without us taking thought.

Again, the Law says that we're successful *now*—not in the future. What this means is that particular lines of force related specifically to you are already in operation on the third-dimensional plane. As part of the Divine Design, the success pattern for you as an individual has already been created. It's filled with opportunities for grand success, and awaits only your understanding of the Law.

What about loving relationships? Same thing—the Law has already deposited in our relationship account the most wonderful experiences possible on the Earth plane. The great Creative Life Force doesn't wait until we're more spiritual, or until we're ready for loving, harmonious relationships. Her Commandment is: "You *must*, by law, be loved and loving."

This includes a circle of friends that will make our hearts sing. True friendship is a sharing relationship, a uniting in mutual understanding, where every opportunity is taken to contribute to each other's well-being. When relations are based on not what we can get but on what we can give, that's when we understand the real meaning of friendship.

And the Law also tells us that the right love-mate is there now—the opportunity for twin flames to burn as one with deep feelings of love and devotion. Remember, if you have a longing for a life partner, it's because you have something special to give to someone—which the other person is seeking. He or she also has a rare gift for you, a quality that will make you feel complete.

The whole thrust of this way of truth-thinking is that the laws of *must-be* (abundance, physical wholeness, success, and loving relations) are written on the heart, in our feeling nature, as the Truth. We have it all and we have it now. We don't have to make anything happen. All we have to do is *know*, which brings us to the third step.

3. Agree with the Law and accept the truth that you have been given everything you could possibly desire in life. When we do this, our consciousness becomes the Law. *I am the law of abundance . . . I am the law of physical perfection . . . I am the law of success . . . I am the law of loving relations. I am the law unto my world, and I must, by law, be rich, whole, successful, and loved.*

With this understanding, we take on the energy, power, and force of the Creative Feminine Principle, and become an open channel for her radiation through us. Are we suddenly rich? Is the body quickly freed of all maladies? Are we instantly recognized for our creative endeavors? Does the right love-mate fall into our arms? It all depends on the degree of agreement and acceptance in consciousness.

What takes place with only a partial or limited agreement and acceptance is similar to a light being turned on in consciousness—ideas begin to fly to the light like moths. These ideas are in the form of helpful solutions, actions to take to bring about relief in the situation. Then once the fear has been quieted through purposeful activity, Creative Mind takes the next step and begins to connect you, through streams of her light, with the people, places, situations, and conditions to bring more of the already-present kingdom into your life. From there, you continue your upward climb until the gifts of the Law are fully recognized.

A complete agreement and acceptance, however, would indeed produce seeming miracles without the limitation of time. The person's life would be dramatically different, with Cause moving directly to effect, Mind into manifestation.

When we begin to work with the idea that *I MUST BE,* the first thing we'll notice is that we're no longer concerned about anything—money, the physical system, our creative self-expression, our relationships. Worry and feelings of unfulfilled desires will fade away, and once this takes place, we'll begin to see things differently. The imaging faculty will open wide, and we'll see not only the possibilities to come, but the realities of *have now,* which will strengthen the faith vibration.

Then, on one particular day, we'll know that we've moved into a new dimension. The first evidence of this may be a tremendous feeling of joy and gratitude. And in the days that follow, we'll realize money from unexpected sources, a heightened sense of well-being mentally and physically, new avenues of success opening up, and a wonderful outpouring of love from people.

A Meditation

Divine Laws are the Principles of Being, the realities of life, the way things are in Truth.

The Law says that scarcity is against the Law, that abundance is natural, and that my finances are continually in a state of all-sufficiency. Regardless of appearances, I accept this Truth.

The Law says my body is whole, vibrant, and well, that radiant health is my true nature. Regardless of appearances, I accept this Truth.

The Law says my success in life is assured, that I am in my true place doing what I love and loving what I do. Regardless of appearances, I accept this Truth.

The Law says my relationships are warm, loving, caring, and meaningful, and that everyone I meet reflects back to me the true spirit of love and goodwill. Regardless of appearances, I accept this Truth.

The Law says that what I accept, I will experience. I have accepted my Truth of Being with all my heart and mind, and I know that by Law, all that is good, true, and beautiful in life is rushing to me now.

The Law is fulfilled, and so am I.

◎ ◎ ◎ ◎ ◎

CHAPTER EIGHT
Where Is Your Consciousness?

Consciousness can be defined as awareness, understanding, and knowledge about any particular aspect of life. We know that we cannot have wealth without a consciousness of abundance; health without a consciousness of wholeness; creative self-expression without a consciousness of success; and right relations without the awareness, understanding, and knowledge of loving relationships.

It's said that every thought is a prayer, that thoughts are things and things are thoughts. We're continually creating our world by our states of consciousness, and I've had people tell me that that's a real downer for them. Reason: When there's scarcity, it's difficult to see the reality of abundance. Same thing for disease, lack of success, and conflict with others. It's hard to see the mountaintop when walking through quicksand.

So what's the answer? Let's look at the idea of abundance and how to find it, then you can apply the process to health, success, and right relations. First of all, we must be *aware* of the Truth of abundance. *Aware* means to be conscious, mindful, alert to. Of what? Of the fact that our Spirit sees us as rich, with unlimited finances for use on the material plane. We were literally financed by God when we came into this incarnation, and more wealth cannot be given, for it's eternally flowing without restriction. Think about this for a moment.

We also become aware of the Divine Design and the great pattern of abundance etched permanently in our energy field with the I AM Identity enfolding it. And we become conscious of the Angel of Abundance, that aspect of Spirit who maintains the Gate of Wealth as an open channel for our supply. Let's do this now.

Next we shift our focus to the omnipresent Mother-Substance, the creative energy of the universe that fills all space, including our force field. This is the Law of Wealth, the Principle of Abundance. While this energy continually flows through our consciousness to provide everything we could ever need, the *intelligence* of that Creative Mind remains within us, listening to our every word (belief). And the word is made flesh (form).

As we become aware of this one Mind in different vibrations, we've taken the first step in developing a consciousness of abundance. Now we must move into understanding. We can be aware of the multiplication table, but unless we understand what it means, it will be of little use to us.

To *understand* means to grasp the meaning of, comprehend, realize—and this is where meditation is so important. We contemplate with ease the truth that our Whole Self wants to express through us as lavish abundance. And this is why "nothing can possibly satisfy anybody short of unlimited supply." Meditate on the idea that it's the Divine Will that you be financed in all your endeavors, always with plenty to spare and share.

After a few moments, focus on the Divine Design in your feeling nature, and meditate on the truth that you've been given the perfect pattern for abundance. Feel the four-sided diamond in your heart center, and use your imaging faculty to bring it into full view. Standing at the upper right angle is the Angel of Abundance, the keeper of the Gate of Wealth, the guardian of the fountain of infinite supply. See her in your mind's eye, and hear her lilting voice as she tells you of your birthright. Shift your attention to Who you are. Your I AM Identity *is* abundance, with no conception whatsoever of lack.

Now think of this universe being filled with Divine Substance. It's present everywhere—it's impossible for scarcity to exist. You literally live, move, and have your being in the Creative Energy of the universe. It's everywhere at once—in, around, and through you—a sea of infinite plenty, throbbing, pulsating, alive. Meditate on the idea of Substance until it becomes real to you. This is the World Mother, the working side of God as Law. See her Presence as a brilliant Light throughout your energy field, and feel her currents as she radiates through your consciousness to manifest and attract visible supply into your life and affairs.

In *Realizing Prosperity,* Franklin Fillmore Farrington writes:

> Man has striven to obtain riches and honor in the form of things and has met with bitter disappointment because he forgot or did not know the truth—that "God is All." One will never have more of Substance but he will have more consciousness of it. The greater a man's consciousness of God, the more things he possesses. You will note I say "possesses." Many people are possessed by their riches instead of possessing the riches. This is because they have had little or no understanding. To me, the word "understanding" means "that which stands under" God as the invisible Substance "stands under"

every form, and to have understanding is to have All, both Substance and form.[1]

Through the meditative exercises shown earlier, understanding will lead to knowledge. You'll *know* that there's always plenty, plenty, plenty—that God's Will is being done through you, and that lack and limitation have been nothing but an illusion. At this point, you'll relax and let the Law prove to you the truth of your abundance. You don't outline how it is to come forth—you simply let God do the work.

THERE'S ALSO ANOTHER WAY TO HAVE THE CONSCIOUSNESS of that which we desire. As I indicated earlier, our I AM is the knowing of lavish abundance, of infinite plenty. It is the manifest Christ vibrating on the frequency of perfect wealth. Recognize the I AM Abundance in your heart. *Be* your Truth. With great love, speak the following:

Now I fully recognize my consciousness of wealth.
(Repeat this three times with purpose of mind)

I call forth my consciousness of plenty to fill my mind with its wealth vibration.
(Repeat this three times, being open and receptive)

Now see and feel a golden mist entering your consciousness and filling it with Divine Awareness, Understanding, and Knowledge of Absolute Abundance. Meditate for a few minutes on this, then say to yourself:

I AM substance.
I AM abundance.
I AM wealth.
I AM the Consciousness of Infinite Plenty.

Your consciousness has now taken on the identity of all-inclusive supply, and the Great Law of the universe always operates on the basis of the identity you are holding up to it. In essence, you have become the supply of Spirit in heart and mind, knowing that the Abundance of the universe is now individualized as you.

Contemplations

My conscious awareness of the Divine Presence as my supply is my supply. I am now consciously aware of the indwelling fountain of overflowing abundance. Therefore, I AM abundant supply. My consciousness is the very energy of money.

I AM the Spirit of Infinite Plenty. I AM boundless abundance, and with love in my heart, I let the universal riches stream forth into perfect manifestation.

What is expressed in love must be returned in full measure. Therefore, wave after wave of visible supply flows to me now. I am wonderfully rich in Mind and manifestation. I now realize my plan for abundant living.

CHAPTER NINE
Act with Bold Authority

W hat follows is an analogy with meaning. You're the
director, and the orchestra is waiting. Are you ready?
The orchestra represents the cosmic energies, the
spiritual forces, the creative medium of the universe, the
Doer. It is the intelligent Mother-Substance of all-inclusive
supply, the receptive Mind of the omnipresent feminine principle of life. It is That which produces all things out of Itself.

Think of the sections of the orchestra as representing
the four primary classifications of the Ideal Life, the Divine
Design. Imagine that the woodwinds with their rich response
are comparable to financial plenty and a life more abundant;
the rhythmic percussion section relates to the tone of wholeness, vitality, and well-being for the physical body; the brass
section with all its different pitches represents creative

success and individual achievement; and the string section with its violins signifies loving and harmonious relationships.

The Divine Design of the Ideal Life is all there, ready to be played by the Divine Musicians as One, according to the full score that you'll write. But remember, you're also the conductor. The "eyes" of the receptive Mind (musicians) are on you and will follow your style, interpretation, and choice of tempo. You lead by means of your baton, hand gestures, facial expressions, and body movements—all of which are symbolic of your authority, command, and focused attention.

Now begin to write your score—your personal symphony that will be played on the stage of life. What are your intentions and aspirations? What can you see? What do you want to compose, create, or orchestrate in your life and affairs? What's your Ideal? Remember that your heartfelt desires are Spirit pressing on you to fulfill those desires. Write your masterpiece.

In order to do this, first turn your attention to the woodwinds and their sounds of lavish abundance. And keep this in mind: Only the notes you write will be the ones played. Don't feel guilty about choosing to have more money. Money is a manifestation of Spirit, and you're deserving of an all-sufficiency of Spirit-in-form. See perfect financial freedom, living completely debt-free and enjoying the fullness of abundance. What is your abundance Ideal? Think/see how you would live with only wholeness and completeness in your financial affairs, and describe the scenario in your journal.

On to the percussion section and the tones of wholeness and radiant health. How do you feel about your physical body? Lift up your vision and see the Truth. Are you willing to be well and strong so that you may live life to the fullest without concern for health? Then accept that Spirit is the only Body, invisible and visible, and in this Reality is only perfection. Capture the image of a body of radiant energy—

vibrant, vital, and whole. And what you see on the inner, you shall become in the outer. Write what you see and feel in your journal.

Now to the brass section and the notes to be played for creative success and right livelihood. What do you want to do for the rest of your life? What do you want to achieve in this lifetime? What creative activities will bring you the greatest happiness? See the Ideal of perfect success, and know that what you see, you shall become. Capture the feeling of achievement, victory, and triumph, and write about it in your journal.

On to the string section and ideal relationships. Look at the people in your life. Are there loving relationships with everyone? Why not? Think of what it would be like to be friends with all the people in this world. And if there's not the perfect love-mate in your life—and you desire such a relationship—why not do what's necessary in consciousness to establish a magnetic attraction? Write in your journal what you can conceive to be your Ideal Life in terms of relationships. Remember, you're writing the score for the orchestra to play.

Before you now is your complete score for all the sections; practice sessions with the orchestra are next in order. But are you an accomplished conductor? Let's take a close look at what's required.

Training to Be the Best Possible Conductor

When you raise your baton with your right hand and stretch forth your left, what are you doing? In essence, you're telling the orchestra to be ready. But are *you* ready? What does the orchestra see? An amateur or a professional? Human or divine? Before you're ready to direct, you must know who you are.

Remember that your Divine Consciousness is an essential unity of masculine and feminine energies. Your Spirit is fully present and expressing as your mind of awareness, your soul—and the Light of I AM has never been extinguished. Turn within to that Light now. From this point of awareness (inward vision), you take on the masculine power of will in spiritual consciousness and behold the infinite orchestra, the Creative Mind of the feminine principle, the One who births all things out of Herself. Yet it's at this point that we seem to have forgotten our role in the scheme of things.

Rather than accepting our role as the conductor, we've been sitting in the audience waiting for our symphony to be played. We've either been relying on someone else to play it for us, or we've assumed that God is going to do something exclusively for us, which only sets up another sense of separation in consciousness. What have we forgotten? The instructions of the ages:

> *Concerning the work of my hands, command ye me.*
> *Boldly tell me what to do and when to act.*
> *Ask what you will.*
> *What do you want me to do for you?*
> *Ask and you shall receive.*
> *Thou shalt decree a thing and it shall be established unto thee.*
> *So shall my word be that goeth forth out of my mouth; it shall not return unto me void, but it shall accomplish that which I please, and it shall prosper in the thing whereto I sent it.*

Pleading prayers, humble petitions, and sitting around and waiting for something to happen aren't implied here. What we're told is to *act with bold authority*—to be the conductors of our lives, the masters of our destinies, the captains of our ships. We know that in spiritual consciousness God's will is our will, so we recognize the one divine will that we are and begin to work with the feminine principle, Mother-Substance, to bring all things to pass.

The Tibetan Master Djwhal Khul tells us that we must become a conscious directing agent in the world of energies and forces: " . . . he creates upon the physical plane that which he desires . . . there is nothing in the created world but energy in motion, and every thought directs some aspects of that energy."[1]

IT IS ALSO IMPORTANT TO KNOW that the Creative Mind of the orchestra is completely impersonal. We might ask, "How do I know if what I contemplate as a part of my Ideal Life is what God thinks is best for me?" The answer is that the manifesting Spirit, the Mothering Aspect of your divinity, doesn't consider what's best for you. Whatever you want as part of your Ideal Life, She leaves up to you, and she will not oppose your decision. However, if your intentions aren't one with the principles of love, peace, and good-for-all, you won't be happy with the outcome. She is to you what you are to Her. Whatever you impress upon her, She expresses accordingly.

Although She will always be impersonal as far as our goals are concerned, as we become more personal to our feminine nature, She will become more personal to us through intuition. In a consciously developed loving relationship with Her, she gives us access to her power of perception, and will prompt us with feelings and ideas that will help us achieve our goals more quickly.

Let's Practice Conducting

The movement of a little finger reaches out through the universe and directly influences the most distant star. This is the ripple effect. Now think what you're doing when you raise your hands to the orchestra—or when you begin your meditative treatment as the conductor with hands outstretched. You're exerting a force in the electromagnetic energy field in and around you. In the pause before movement, you're balancing the energies, exercising your will, and bringing your concentration to bear on what you're doing. This sends a message to the magnetic energy of the Divine Mother within that you're ready to begin.

And as you do, the movement of your hands and body and your facial expressions relate to your thoughts of truth and words of power. Remember that thoughts and words by themselves aren't omnipotent—rather, it's the *consciousness* behind the thoughts and words that give them power.

**Now, focus on the woodwinds
in the orchestra with these words:**

In the Pure Being I AM, and with Thought Divine, I speak the truth. I am the wealth of the universe in individual expression; therefore, I am very rich. I always have abundance for I am the Law of Infinite Plenty. I live the Abundance Ideal.

To the percussion section, say:

In the Pure Being I AM, and with Thought Divine, I speak the truth. I am the wholeness of the universe in individual expression; therefore, every cell, tissue, and organ of my body is in a state of divine order and perfect well-being. I always enjoy radiant health, for I am the Law of Purity and Perfection unto my body. I live the Body Ideal.

To the brass section, say:

In the Pure Being I AM, and with Thought Divine, I speak the truth. I am the success of the universe in individual expression; therefore, my every activity is completely successful, and I go forth each day to achieve and accomplish in accordance with my highest vision. I am the Law of Victory and Triumph. I live the Success Ideal.

To the string section, say:

In the Pure Being I AM, and with Thought Divine, I speak the truth. I am the love and harmony of the universe in individual expression; therefore, I enjoy only beautiful and loving relationships with everyone. I have wonderful friends, the perfect life partner, and totally harmonious relations with all. I am the Law of Love unto my world. I live the Relationship Ideal.

Now bring out the whole score you've written, the vision of how you want your life to be in each area. Read the words that you wrote in your journal as you contemplated your Ideal Life. Feel it. Get the highest and clearest vision. Purposely with will, dismiss all conditional thoughts such as time, how it will be accomplished, or any other limiting factors lingering in consciousness from the past. Focus only on the WHAT with great clarity and feeling.

To the orchestra, which is symbolic of the great Creative Mind of the universe, say:

These are my intentions; this is how I want to live my life. I ask that you play this symphony in glorious harmony as one with my consciousness. Let us begin.

As you move with the dynamic flow of energies, *hear* the symphony of your life being played with the majesty of celestial sounds. *See* every image as real and revel in it. *Feel* the NOW of what you see, remembering that the Creative Principle has no conception of time.

And when the symphony has been played with ears to hear and eyes to see, smile and take a bow. The audience of angels from every kingdom is applauding. You are a master composer and conductor.

Go about your day now in peace and with joyous thanksgiving.

CHAPTER TEN

The Dance of Life

Time for a change of pace. Shall we dance? *Dance:* Rhythmical steps and motions. *Life:* Livingness; living fully with vitality, spirit, zest. Put them together, add music (harmony) . . . and you have the Dance of Life.

You may love to dance—to swing, sway, twirl, and shake for the joy of it. But the key is to carry the feeling and flow into life itself. When you dance, the focus is narrowed to let your body, mind, and spirit become one with the cadence, time, and rhythm of the music. And when you dance with life—to the universal beat of abundance, perfect health, creative self-expression, and loving relationships—you follow the same process.

Let's look again at the four basic patterns of life, the Divine Design.

Financial All-Sufficiency

You can't get money. It's the other way around—money is constantly striving to get *you*, to give of itself, but you put up a barrier by worrying about it. So money asks, "Why do you worry about me? You treat me like a lost little kid, but I'm just fine. Quit being anxious. Open your arms and receive me. Come on, let's dance together."

Money is happy, always smiling. It loves what it does, what it buys, and the pleasures it gives. After all, money is the energy of love in visible form. Its energy is feminine; its root is eternal goodness. In *The Abundance Book,* I wrote: "By working with the rhythmic Energy of Self, whatever form that was needed for exchange (the legal tender at the time) was brought forth as an instrument of *goodwill.* As such, 'money' was simply a token of appreciation of one's service, a symbol of love and integrity."[1]

The Source of energy-to-be-form is Mother-Substance, the energy that appears as money. And the perfect pattern for the manifestation of money is in the Divine Design, overshadowed by the Angel of Abundance. Bring her into your heart, into your feeling nature, and listen to her music. It's a love song. Dance with her as she sings to you, knowing that the energy flowing through your oneness will open every door to let money in. And as it does, and you begin to feel richer and richer, dance with that feeling.

Now think on these thoughts:

There is always abundance everywhere, and I now let it manifest in my life. I am open to receive.

I cannot be limited, for I am the Spirit of Infinite Plenty. I am the Shining Sun of Supply, and God's wealth fills my world.

Catch the vibration. Hear the music of abundance. Move in step with it, and you'll understand why Louise Hay says that money is the easiest thing to demonstrate. It is, when you dance with abundance. When you move in oneness with that energy, beliefs in lack and limitation—the only thing that's limiting you—are transformed.

Wholeness of Body

When you dance to the beat of radiant well-being, you're honoring your perfection, your truth. You don't *get* health from what you eat or don't eat; you don't *get* sick from something "out there." There's nothing "out there" to cause anything. It's all consciousness, and your body is a reflection of what you're thinking and feeling. Nothing in the phenomenal world *causes* allergies, arthritis, asthma, cancer, diabetes, hemorrhoids, or warts. The energy from which all form comes forth (and that includes microscopic organisms) is neutral, harmless. There's no power in effects. It's the identity you're living—a limited concept of yourself—that misdirects and alters the energy and attracts these and other maladies.

But understand this: On some level of your consciousness, right at this moment, you know it's impossible to experience anything but perfection. You know that illness is a lie because the Presence of God is as you now. Can God be diseased? No! And that song of wholeness is being played throughout your energy field, the truth etched permanently in your heart center. Listen. The melody is so beautiful. When you consciously dance with the truth of perfection, you transcend the experience of disease. When you get positively excited about life, life gets positively excited about you, for the law of life is one of correspondence.

Think on these thoughts:

I see myself with a magnificently healthy body in perfect order, where every cell is in the image of the perfect pattern, and I am whole and complete.

I see myself as vibrant, energetic, and filled with a new zest for life. I feel wonderful!

Feel the rhythm of these thoughts and words. Become one with the vibration of the Angel of Truth and Enlightenment, let it come forth as music, and let your body move with the melody. Dance with the Angel; dance with Life. And watch what happens to your physical system.

True Success

Don't equate success with money. You'll always have money when you live the Abundance Identity. What I'm talking about now is the creative activity of loving what you do and doing what you love in a spirit of achievement and accomplishment.

It may be as simple as growing flowers, creating beauty in the home, or in my case, writing books. With your New Thought, you've got many more years to live on planet Earth, so what are you going to do? Will you have Success to dance with?

Right now, you're filled with success because you have the perfect pattern of success along with the angel who maintains it. This angel is part of you, and lives in an aura of magnificent creative accomplishment within your energy field. This is masculine energy, and he loves to dance. Ask this Angel of Success to come into your feeling nature. Feel the warmth and the vibration, and let the music play. Feel the movement of success in your body, and begin the dance.

Think on these thoughts:

I am enjoying the fullness of unlimited success, for I am the spirit of accomplishment, the force of achievement.

Every activity of my life now reflects only victory, beauty, and harmony. I live the Success Ideal.

Catch the vibration. Hear the music. And while you're dancing, think about what creative activity in life would give you the greatest pleasure—what would you truly love to do?

Loving Relationships

Isn't this what we all want? This urge is simply the pressing of Universal Law upon us, telling us that loving relationships, from the most intimate kind all the way out to friendly, smiling strangers, is the natural process of life.

To ensure that we'd always live in love and harmony with people, we were given that perfect pattern, always protected by the Angel of Loving Relationships. This Archetype living within us represents the life force of masculine and feminine energies, opposites bonded together and complementing each other as one specialized Causal Power. Bring this Living Energy into your feeling nature, and pick up the vibration. Such beautiful music emanates from that loving presence. Listen, hear the beat, and let it flow into your body. Begin the dance.

In your oneness with this music of the spheres, you're blocking out all thoughts and emotions that could repel love, goodwill, harmony, and meaningful friendships. And you're accepting and approving of yourself, because *you* are that angel. When you dance with that aspect of your Self in a spirit of love, you're sending out vibrations in an ever-widening circle, which will return to you as your heart's desire.

Think on these thoughts:

Love is the greatest power in the universe, freely given to one and all.

God loves me, and through God's love, I can love others.

As I love others, I am loved.

My harmonious thoughts are returned in kind. What I am feeling about another, I am feeling about myself. I choose to only feel peacefully and lovingly toward all.

What I want for myself, I want for everyone. I practice harmlessness in thought and feeling each and every day.

Move into that feeling and sense its vibration. There's a beat there. Get into the flow. Through the dance, you become a mighty magnet for all right relations.

It's amazing what happens when we truly enjoy the Dance of Life.

CHAPTER ELEVEN

Let It Be Done

Those of us on the spiritual path have tried so hard to bring our lives up to the divine standard, and have used every spiritual tool we've found in books or heard about in workshops to grow more fruit on our vines. We've affirmed and spoken the word, imagined and visualized, treated and prayed, meditated and practiced the Presence, forgiven seventy times seven and released the guilt to Spirit, journaled questions and listened for the answers, thought positively and felt powerfully, worked with the angels and called on spiritual guides, wrote new spiritual contracts and tossed the old ones, and practiced nonjudgment and unconditional love—sometimes with clenched teeth.

And we've made some progress along the way. But are we "there" yet? Maybe it's time to stop pressing and let Spirit have

Its own way with us—to relax more, get loose, and let the Divine Plan be revealed in all its glory. It could be that we've been so focused on trying to make things happen spiritually that we've actually impeded the creative activity of Spirit. This preoccupation with satisfying the wants of life through what we consider spiritual mind-action may have taken us out of the stream of the *natural process,* where everything is already being done as the will, way, word, and work of God. Let's go the *way* of the Lord-God-Self and become an instrument for Spirit. Let it be done.

In 1923, Franklin Fillmore Farrington wrote:

> This Universal Mind pervades every atom of man and thinks by means of him, using him as a fit instrument. The desire which you have from within is the manifestation of the great universal Intelligence, craving expression through you and by means of you. Expression is Life (God); repression is death. As you realize that this urge is really not from your conscious mind, but from the great Within, you will realize the importance of relaxation. As long as we believe that the desire for prosperity, health and happiness is from man's mind, just so long will we rush about and worry, endeavoring to fulfill those desires. However, when we realize that we have nothing to do but to "let" the great universal Mind express itself through us, then will we relax mentally.
>
> We need to keep open for the "inflow" and the "outflow." We may conclude that desire in the heart is God knocking at the door of our consciousness with His Infinite Supply. It is well to remember that supply always precedes demand. Universal Energy as Mind, Life, Love, Truth and Substance is always trying to pour more of itself through us into visibility. The word "express" comes from "ex," out of, and "premere," [*sic*] to press out, so that the

statement, "God expresses Himself through Man" means "God presses Himself out through Man"—as He does through every visible thing.

We must remember that we have nothing to do with the working of the law, but we have some conscious part in just how the law will work. God as the Universal Energy flows on and on as silent, impersonal, Omnipotent Power until it reaches a place where consciousness is manifest.[1]

Let's also remember the trinity of Being: Father, Mother, Son (Sun). The Father Spirit doesn't think, It *Knows*. It is the unconditionally loving Presence of God, Who sees us as perfect in every aspect and activity of life. In that Divine Vision is the fullness of a life more abundant—financial plenty, radiant health, true success, and loving relationships. And the Vision is Will, the dynamic urge for Its Self-expression to be and have all that is felt in heart and imaged in mind. And the Will is done.

Mother-Substance *thinks* as creative Intelligence. This Aspect of God is the Wisdom of the Ages, the Divine Activity as the Law of Will, and there's nothing It cannot do. All space is filled with this Energy, so there's no void or separation. Neither is there time, so there's no consciousness of delay. All is now. This Intelligent Substance is ready to create a whole new life for you based on the Love, Vision, and Will of the Supreme I AM. It is all-pressing on you now as what you consider your personal desires, yet in truth the desires are the Intentions of Spirit for Self-expression through you.

Substance vibrates to our every thought and word. We think and speak into it, and it responds accordingly. To have a prosperity consciousness means that we know there is plenty of God, of Substance. Same thing for health, success, and right relations. We must have the consciousness of Intelligent Substance before we can have the desirable forms and experience. If we concentrate only on getting the money, healing the body, achieving a particular goal, or harmonizing a relationship, we're emphasizing a sense of have *not*. But when we focus on and realize the all-inclusive Mother Substance, we become in a vibration of *have*.

Franklin Fillmore Farrington continues:

> There is always Substance enough to make more than you ever desired, but you have to believe in more than you see and that all things visible have come out of the invisible. We are walking through this invisible "something"— living in it, breathing it, thinking into it, talking into it, and according to our thoughts and words shall the Substance be formed. The material is here. If you think negatively, you will have negative results. If you think and speak positively into this universal Substance, you will have positive results.[2]

Your personal consciousness, the *Chooser*, is the channel for the Divine Currents, and in the heart of the soul-sun you are is the manifest I AM, the Identity of the highest vibration on the physical plane. And remember the Divine Agents, the angels within, who work with the I AM to condition consciousness for the natural process of expression.

Choose now to fully identify with this Truth of your being and Its Divine Design, and not with the world "out there." Thoughts and words must correspond to the I AM Truth, the original Idea of God, otherwise the power is neutralized.

The I AM within *is* the identity of wealth, therefore, *I AM Wealth.*

The I AM within *is* the identity of wholeness, therefore, *I AM Perfect Health.*

The I AM within *is* the identity of success, therefore *I AM Success.*

The I AM within *is* the identity of right relations, therefore, *I AM Loving Relationships.*

This opens the channel for the inflow and the outflow, and what we call "miracles" become the norm. The flow of Substance takes place through a coordinate in our energy field corresponding to the solar plexus and heart centers. This is where the manifested Christ-I AM encircles the Divine Design, the perfect patterns for manifestation. Pause for a moment and feel the energy moving in and through you to appear as substantial form. From Cause to effect, all is energy. The Giver and the gift are one as the Invisible becomes visible.

Vitvan, founder of the School of the Natural Order, put it this way:

> As you go about your daily living, remember that "matter" is merely a word meaning ENERGY. (In fact, *matter* is a word meaning Mother-energy . . . *matter* is derived from the word *mater* meaning *mother*.) Whether your work is as a housewife at home, or in an office, store, workshop, studio, classroom—whatever you do—wherever you are— get into the *energy* orientation.
>
> Whatever you touch—whatever you look at, say: "This is called energy. This represents energy in configuration. This represents a dynamic energy process."
>
> In this age we do not deal with THINGS and OBJECTS—we deal with ENERGY. Never think in terms of THING, but think in terms of ENERGY.[3]

Understand that this way of thinking will soon condition consciousness to the truth of plenty, plenty, plenty, everywhere. The key is indeed *understanding.* Following the theme of the Farrington papers, let's continue with understanding as our goal.

IN A PREVIOUS CHAPTER, I talked about false beliefs. Another way to eliminate those beliefs is to deny them. I know that many on the path don't favor denials. They feel that when you declare that something is untrue, you're bringing that something more firmly into consciousness. This is possible if the process isn't done properly. First, you must understand the truth that Mind, Substance, and Energy fills all space; therefore, no vacancies exist in the infinite nature of God. Next, think of yourself carrying on a conversation with someone. You explain, "Since the abundance of God is everywhere, there cannot be any lack. And because the creative energy of success is omnipresent, there's no failure in the universal scheme of things. Lack and failure are nothing but false beliefs projected on the screen of life, but they have no reality—therefore, they don't exist in Mind."

From this, we see that denials do not trigger negative emotions. Rather, they set us free. Now speak the truth slowly and audibly:

All is God everywhere present. There is no place where God is not. Therefore . . .
> *There is no lack, anywhere.*
> *There is no imperfection, anywhere.*
> *There is no failure, anywhere.*
> *There is no conflict, anywhere.*
> *There is no criticism, anywhere.*
> *There is no injustice, anywhere.*
> *There is no fear, anywhere.*
> *There is no delay, anywhere.*

Can you believe this? If God, Mind, Spirit, or Substance (all meaning the same thing) fills all space, then there's nothing in this universe and our individual energy fields except perfect harmony and divine order. As I said, anything else is but a false belief (which we made up) and can be dissolved through persistent denials.

Now let's look at affirmations. To affirm the demonstration of form—that which we can see—lowers the vibration of our energy field and has but a temporary affect on conditions. For example, a concentration on "money" in affirmative prayer can actually be counterproductive to our intent. However, when we affirm in a consciousness of Spirit, focusing on the invisible, the vibration moves to a higher level, and we see positive— and lasting—results.

Farrington writes: "Things that are seen are low vibration; the unseen (abundant substance) is high vibration. Think God (Life, Light, Love, Mind, Intelligence, Spirit, Substance, Power, Truth, Success—formless) and you are at the threshold of Supply."[4]

A Treatment for Completeness in Life

Sit up straight in your chair, feet flat on the floor. Take several deep breaths and relax . . . relax . . . . relax. With eyes closed, feel the stream of Light from the Universal I AM above your crown chakra, extending Itself to a point between your heart and solar plexus chakras. See with your mind's eye, and feel the focus of that Beam as the Truth within, the *Knower* in expression as the manifest Christ. Slowly move into that I AM Presence within. Be consciously aware that the I AM is at the center of your being, and you are in that center.

Lift your gaze now to the source of the Light above, and say, "I AM *That* I AM." Repeat this three times. Now follow the stream of Light back down to the center of your being, and repeat three times: "All that my Divine Consciousness is, I AM. All that my Divine Consciousness has, is mine. I AM the Divine Design for my life."

Now think of God-Substance, Creative Intelligence, everywhere present, and say, "There is no lack. There is no lack of anything. There is no lack of anything, anywhere." Ponder what you've said for a moment, and let understanding come through.

Now speak these words slowly, audibly:

> *There is always plenty.*
> *There is always plenty, everywhere.*
> *There is always plenty of Substance.*
> *Abundance is everywhere.*
> *Wholeness and perfection are everywhere.*
> *Success is everywhere.*
> *Love is everywhere.*
> *I live and move and have my being in universal*
>   *Substance.*
> *I AM this Creative Energy.*
> *I AM the Law.*
> *I AM Abundance.*
> *I AM Health.*
> *I AM Success.*
> *I AM Loved and Loving.*

Move into the dynamic vibration of this Truth. *Feel* it. Now think again about those pressing desires—how Spirit wants to express through you. Do this now, and speak your desires audibly, knowing that what you desire, you already *have*.

Next, go into the Silence and meditate for ten to fifteen minutes on Substance. See and feel yourself in a sea of omnipresent, vibrating Substance. Breathe Substance. Feel your energy field filled with Substance. See yourself living in Substance, moving in Substance. Sense the rhythmic activity of this Creative Intelligence in, around, and through you.

Keep your mind focused on the Great Invisible filling all space, beyond all time.

Now meditate deeply on these truths:

I am the open channel through which Substance is flowing as wealth (pause for contemplation).

I am the open channel through which Substance is flowing as health (pause and feel the flow of wholeness).

I am the open channel through which Substance is flowing as creative self-expression (pause and contemplate the river of success moving through you).

I am the open channel through which Substance is flowing as loving relationships (pause and let the love shine through).

Change your focus now and become aware of the very Spirit of God you are, the Christ, *in* your consciousness, closer than breathing. It is your consciousness *of* Spirit that appears *as* total fulfillment in your life. Spend several minutes in this Self-contemplation.

As you come back into personal consciousness, speak the Word audibly:

All of my desires are now fulfilled in Substance. I relax. I let go. I let it be done.

There is no more struggle. It *is* done. The only thing you are to do now is to follow the lead of Spirit, to take action based on your intuitive guidance. And remember . . .

*You will not need to fight in this battle; take your
    position, stand still, and see the victory of the
    Lord on your behalf.*
*Stand still, and see the salvation of the Lord,
    which He will show to you.*
Be still, and know that I am God.
Fret not.
*Thou dost keep Him in perfect peace, Whose mind
    is stayed on thee.*
The government shall be upon His shoulder.

This letting go and surrendering to Spirit—after we've
done our work to purify, condition, and strengthen consciousness—means to become an instrument through which
Spirit works to fulfill Itself, thus bringing Heaven to Earth. I
had a personal experience that showed me the true meaning
of this:

I was shown a house, and was told that I *was* the
house. My attention was then directed to a wall in the
house. As I was staring at the wall, a large hole appeared
and I could see through to the outside. Then what seemed
to be a large firehose was elevated to the position of the hole
and water started pouring through. Watching the steady
stream, I heard . . . "I am a hole in the wall bearing witness to the flow. The water represents the Activity, the
Word, the flow of Knowingness into manifestation of whatever is needed in my life. I cannot use or possess the
water . . . I of myself can do nothing but be aware. The flow
represents the All Good of the Universe, and yet, even
while it pours through me, I cannot call myself good, rich,
whole, or perfect. To do so would call for the possibility of
experiencing evil, lack, limitation, and imperfection. That
is polarity, and there are no opposites in the Mind of God.

Therefore, I can only BE—and I die daily to the thought of having anything but the water, the Spirit of God, and the flow, the Activity of Spirit."[5]

Catch the meaning of this. Our responsibility is to be a channel for Spirit—to keep the channel open and witness the beautiful manifestations of Spirit. This is God fulfilling Itself on Earth as in Heaven without our interference. And the part that says "I cannot call myself good, rich, whole, or perfect" is a reminder that we must keep our minds and hearts anchored in the Invisible Essence of Cause rather than the effects. We must *be* that which Spirit is expressing—goodness, abundance, wholeness, and perfection.

Look Now at Faith

Faith (Peter) was one of the first spiritual faculties/disciples Jesus called forth. And the reason is that faith is our consciousness—our consciousness is our faith. If we're placing our faith in insufficiency, in the inevitability of sickness, in the possibility of failure, or in the darkness of conflict, that's what will be outpictured in our lives. So our Example showed us that in order to have the complete life, we must have faith as our foundation.

In the *Metaphysical Bible Dictionary*, Charles Fillmore wrote: "You are the free will, the directive ego, Jesus. . . . You are the high priest without beginning of years or end of days, the alpha and the omega; but you cannot do what the Father has set before you without disciplining your powers. Your thinking faculty (faith) is the first to be considered. It is the inlet and the outlet of all your ideas."[6]

I had a dream one night that dealt with faith. A group of us were lined up and moving toward the entrance to a great cathedral. A man walked up to me and said, "John, let Peter move in front of you." I stepped back and let him enter the line. I really didn't realize the significance of the dream until I read later in the *Metaphysical Bible Dictionary:* "Keep your eye on Peter. Make him toe the line every moment."[7]

I hadn't been focusing my attention on the faith faculty, which, as I wrote in *The Superbeings,* is "the power that can unite all the other powers in a perfect pattern of mastery and dominion . . . faith is the connecting link between heaven and earth, between cause and effect. The incredibly awesome force of this power will penetrate into the depths of consciousness and burn away the hardened strata of error thought (fear and unbelief)."[8]

Let's keep faith at the forefront of our consciousness as we intensify our awareness of our Spirit-Source, our understanding of the Gifts—the Divine Patterns—and our knowledge of the mighty waters of Creative Mind flowing eternally to express the Truth of our Being.

One highly effective way to strengthen our conscious awareness of the Presence—and thus our faith in our own Reality—is to let our Holiness think/speak through us. The *how* of this process is discussed in the next chapter.

CHAPTER TWELVE
Lessons from Within

In *With Wings As Eagles*, I wrote about contemplative meditation to get in tune with the Presence within as the ultimate Teacher: "If there are only feelings and symbols at first, ask yourself, 'What do I intuitively feel that Spirit is saying to me?'—and write what comes into your mind. Meditate, listen, write. Meditate, listen, write."[1]

Here are the results of one such process from several years ago. The messages were given to me in specific points over a period of time, 45 in all. Later I separated the messages into "Five Nines" and realized that 4 + 5 = 9, the number of *completion*.

Relax, open your mind, and slowly contemplate each message for greater understanding.

I

1. From the one Light shines countless Lights, forever one in the Light, individual in thought yet blended in unity.

2. Purity is thy name, pure life, pure will, pure being, coming from the invisible world and creating form in the visible.

3. But the sleep of isolation fell upon you, and you remember not, and love not, and know not, yet the light flashes and you are stirring.

4. You have believed falsely, and the false world mirrors that belief. Let the mirror be shattered.

5. You see conflict and scarcity, illusions in mind made manifest as false reality, to which you respond with fear.

6. Fear supports and enlarges the illusion, prompting fearful actions that lead to guilt and the concept of punishment.

7. Guilt inspires judgment of others as less than perfect, which is nothing more than a reflection of self. Do not honor the lie of imperfection. See only truth.

8. See with true vision beyond the form, to the Essence of One Who is All forever in shining expression, and know only oneness throughout creation.

9. You are Spirit forever one with the One Who is the All, which is pure love.

II

1. Can you not depend on God Who loves you? God is love and love is the essence of all things visible and invisible, the foundation of Life itself.

2. Life as true living without fear begins in your world through forgiveness. To forgive is to cease judging. To judge is to deny who and what you are.

3. Denial of Self produces needs where there were none. Knowledge of Self eliminates the needs, for Self is the principle of fulfillment.

4. To know your Self is to know the One Who is All, for the One is All there is. All is the One Presence knowing of Itself.

5. The image of yourself hides the truth of you. Change the image from form to Spirit, from the visible to the Invisible, and you see rightly.

6. When you see rightly, your creative powers are released, not to change the world but to change yourself. Seek not to heal the world. Heal yourself.

7. You change yourself through love, for love is the correcting principle, the power that dissolves the illusion of separation.

8. You cannot be separate from the One Who is the All and continue to live, for the One is your life and you are eternal, immortal.

9. Know yourself as everyone, and see everyone as your light, and your darkness will be no more.

III

1. What you do to anyone in thought, word, or deed, you do to yourself. To attack another is to attack yourself. To love another is to love yourself.

2. Love created you, and your creations shall be of love, otherwise they are illusions speaking of needs.

3. A mind in need manipulates to fulfill the need, as nothing attempts to create nothing from nothing, a useless attempt.

4. You can think and speak from darkness or light. The first is from your perception of the world of form. The second is from your knowing of your true Self.

5. Light can be frightening to those who have lived only in darkness, and can be perceived as a loss of control, but darkness controls only in fear.

6. You are Spirit who has lived forever in the Light; it was the mask you donned that blocked the vision.

7. Open your mind to the Light within, and you will be shown the path to remembrance. The lighted path rises inwardly.

8. Your true nature thinks thoughts of perfect harmony. Think with Spirit, and false thoughts will be erased, as will your miscreations.

9. Love created you, yet you created repulsion. Be willing to let the illusions you created be corrected by Spirit.

IV

1. The One Who is All loves you. The Mind of the Infinite is forever on you, thinking you, loving you, caring for you.

2. There is no separation between your mind and the One Mind. It is Light shining as Light, Fire manifesting as Fire, Love expressing as Love. You are part of God.

3. Illness is an illusion made real by fearful mind speaking to the body, yet the body does not hear. Only the mind is ill.

4. Your personality has a higher and lower vibration. The higher resonates with Spirit, with Truth, the lower with fear and falsity.

5. The higher mind of personality as God-Light maintains your identity as an individual and listens to the knowing of Spirit as complete fulfillment.

6. The lower self-created emotional mind of personality maintains the illusion of a physical being forever seeking the fulfillment of needs.

7. Joy is your natural state. Let the mind hold on to the joyousness of Spirit and partake of that essence. What you observe within, you become.

8. Joy and sadness cannot exist simultaneously. When you choose one, the other cannot be. Choose joy and leave the other in the wake.

9. Everyone deserves joy and love because all are deservingly innocent. There is no rationale in the universe for guilt.

V

1. Never fear the One Who is the All, for in the All there is nothing to fear. Shall you fear love and life, joy and peace?

2. Change your mind about everyone, whether perceived as good or evil. See all with a new understanding of the pure holiness of their being.

3. Forgive everyone for everything. Release all from your condemnation, and you will be released.

4. Never judge anyone for their actions. It is *you* who judges, for the lights are merged and you are seeing yourself.

5. A problem cannot be solved in the humanly created world. Temporary relief is never a permanent solution. Forgive the world and break the spell of harmfulness.

6. Find one person in the world you can love and forgive, one person whom you can see as completely innocent, and you will awaken to the truth of your being.

7. Every person on Earth exists right where you are. Souls are united as one, one Spirit, omnipresent in nonspace.

8. Scarcity in any form will vanish throughout the world when the collective mind recognizes that all Souls are one and united in the One called God.

9. When scarcity vanishes, so will the illusions of the world. It will be the end of the old and the beginning of the new, a time of gladness and great celebration.

Turn within now to the one Teacher. Feel that Presence of Love within and around you, and invite your Master Self to think through you. Don't try to control your thoughts, for that may result in mental conflict. Simply surrender to Higher Mind, and affirm: "The Spirit I AM is now using my mind to think, and I am totally receptive to the word." Meditate, listen, and write what comes through.

Your journal could very well become *your* Book of Life.

CHAPTER THIRTEEN
Things to Think About

In the previous chapters, we looked at the New Thought teachings, studied the "missing link"—that God is expressed AS each individual being, which led us to discover our Divine Constitution, the Divine Design for our lives, and the loving assistance from the Master Builders. We realized that we were the Law unto our world, checked the tone and pitch of our consciousness, exercised our authority, and danced with life to get into the rhythm of the natural process. Then, with a greater understanding of God, life, and this world—and a treatment for Completeness—we relaxed, let go, and let Spirit fulfill Itself in and through us. And we continued our journey by turning to Spirit, our Holy Self, as the inner Teacher.

So what's the next step? I believe that it's to free our minds of any confusion in certain controversial areas—to clear our consciousness from emotional blips that could retard our progress on the path. Example: I was on one of those call-in radio shows, and the host asked about my views on reincarnation. My response set off an immediate firestorm. The first caller admonished me because reincarnation is not mentioned in the Bible; therefore, it cannot be true. Another pointed out that even some New Thought teachings deny the concept of rebirth.

Let's begin here to clear up confusion on this and other button-pushing topics; then we'll look at spreading happiness around, review reminders of our Truth of Being, and move on into Part II with the fruits of the harvest—where *nothing is too good to be true, nothing is too wonderful to happen.*

An Overview of Reincarnation

All of the sacred academies taught the principle of rebirth as an expression of the will aspect of the soul. This was echoed in the Hindu religion, particularly in the Bhagavad Gita, as reincarnation and not transmigration—the latter meaning the possibility of returning to Earth in the body of an animal, which would be against the law of the cosmic process. And 500 years before Jesus, Buddha taught the cycle of return to his students; it was also accepted by the Jews. The Essenes—teachers of John the Baptist and Jesus— believed in the law of rebirth as well. This means that it was an accepted teaching of the early Christians.

Look at Matthew 17:10–13: "And the disciples asked him, 'Then why do the scribes say that first Elijah must come?' He replied, 'Elijah does come, and he is to restore all things; but I tell you that Elijah has already come, and they did not know him, but did to him whatever they pleased. So also the Son of man will suffer at their hands.' Then the disciples understood that he was speaking to them of John the Baptist."

There were other biblical teachings, and the Gnostic tracts of the first century were filled with dialogues on the law of rebirth. However, in the sixth century, the synod of Constantinople removed from the Bible most of the references to reincarnation, but that didn't stop the leading Christian theologians such as St. Augustine and St. Francis of Assisi from stating their positive views. And of course we had Voltaire, Goethe, Shelley, Schopenhauer, Emerson, Whitman, Browning, Tennyson, and Cayce—to name only a few who believed strongly in progressive unfoldment through the law of rebirth.

Let's remember that returning to the Earth plane is a conscious decision on our part—it's a positive experience, not a negative one. In fact, some of us reincarnate for the pure joy of it, as a service to help turn this world around. For another reason, we have to go back to "the beginning." According to the message I received while writing *With Wings As Eagles,* reincarnation was not originally a part of the Cosmic System. But ". . . once the earliest Souls were freed to return to the higher plane, there was an awareness that *the original perfection of man could only be regained in the vibration where the ideal state was lost—the energy of Earth.* Thus, the spiritual collective established the Law of Rebirth. It is now a part of what you may call the Law of Evolution."[1]

One teaching states that the soul returns again and again to Earth, to learn all that the school of life has to teach, just as the child returns to school day after day and year after year until he graduates. Why do some people consider that so terrible? Yes, we can choose to remain on the other side for eternity in a state of Cosmic Consciousness—once our entire belief system is purified. But in the meantime, we continue the perfecting process *where the ideal state was lost.* In other words, if I lost a sack of diamonds in the desert, I wouldn't go to the mountains to find it.

Emogene S. Simons, author of a study course in Theosophy, writes:

> Reincarnation provides a basis for the . . . vast inequalities on every hand—the varying circumstances into which we are born, for example—in one case into ease, in another into hardship and privation; in one case to loving parents, in another to a childhood of neglect; in one case with physical beauty, in another disfigured or deformed; in one case a genius, in another perhaps an idiot. Heredity does not supply the reason for the almost unending variations in circumstances, talents, capacities, abilities.[2]

In *The Other Side of Death,* Jan Price says:

> The fact that I had lived many times in physical form was made very clear to me. This was not a surprise, for I had been given glimpses of other lives over the years. . . . Why am I including the idea of reincarnation in this book? Three reasons. First, to emphasize again that once we leave this plane via the death process, we do not become suddenly illumined as master teachers. We take our consciousness with us, and continue in the same mind-set and belief system that we had on earth. Second, to show that living in the "heavenly realm" does not mean a fast-forwarding of the evolutionary process into overnight enlightenment. That's simply not the natural process. And the third reason is to show that through reincarnation, we can learn, grow, and eventually return in consciousness to an awakening of our divine nature.[3]

The Hell Thing

The fear of death and what lies beyond among critically ill hospital patients was the subject of a recent newspaper article. I've also heard talk about people being "hellbound" or "surely going to hell to be punished" for something they've done. And there was a column written by a well-known religious figure saying that "the reward of Heaven or the punishment of everlasting hell awaits us when we die." The ignorance and absurdity of this in today's more enlightened world baffles me.

Hell as an eternal afterlife punishment wasn't even mentioned as a possibility in the early religions, or in the old Sacred Academies and Mystery Schools. It was originally introduced as a warning by Moses to the Hebrews, and the concept was carried over into the New Testament. Professional researcher Barbara G. Walker writes:

> [Hell] was perhaps the most sadistic fantasy ever conceived by the mind of man. It was described, painted, and contemplated with incredibly perverse relish. . . . In wrestling with the problem of God's responsibility for hell, theologians of the 17th and 18th centuries often found themselves forced by their own logic into a basically Manichean image of an evil God. . . . [one of the theologians concluded that] the very existence of hell must condemn God in the eyes of humanity.[4]

The Authorized King James Version of the Bible says that "two words are translated in the New Testament by 'hell,' namely, 'Hades' and 'Gehenna.' 'Hades' is the Latin translation of 'Sheol' and means literally 'the unseen world' . . . 'unseen because it is a temporary level of consciousness and not a particular location for so-called lost souls." Continuing, the Bible reports that "Gehenna (from the valley of Hinnom) was the place for burning the refuse of the city, dead animals, and the bodies of criminals."

It appears that the Bible revisionists in the fourth century used the word *hell* as an abode of punishment, rather than saying that evildoers could experience a state of mind and body comparable to the smoldering fire of a city dump. Not dramatic enough, so they rewrote the original texts to bring in this damnation business to instill fear and guilt in the hearts and minds of the masses for greater church control.

Tibetan Master Djwhal Khul says:

> Christianity has emphasized immortality but has made eternal happiness dependent upon the acceptance of a theological dogma: Be a true professing Christian and live in a somewhat fatuous Heaven or refuse to be an accepting Christian, or a negative professing Christian, and go to an impossible hell, a hell growing out of the theology of The Old Testament and its presentation of a God full of hate and jealousy. Both concepts are today repudiated by all sane, sincere, thinking people. No one of any true reasoning power or with any true belief in a God of love accepts the heaven of the churchmen or has any desire to go there. Still less do they accept the "lake that burneth with fire and brimstone" or the everlasting torture to which a God of love is supposed to condemn all who do not believe in the theological interpretations of the Middle Ages, or the modern fundamentalists, or of the unreasoning churchmen who seek—through doctrine, fear and threat—to keep people in line with the obsolete old teaching.[5]

In *The Other Side of Death,* Jan speaks from a deeply personal experience beyond the veil:

I've been asked what I learned about "religion." For one thing, there is not an angry God, a literal hell, or a valley of sorrows where we are punished for our sins. Man-made religion came up with this idea, and it is a false one. . . . Teachings that hold fear over the heads of followers deny a God of love and create great anxiety about the qualifications for entrance through their heavenly gate.[6]

There is also Edwin Steinbrecher's death-and-return experience, as reported in his book, *The Inner Guide Meditation:*

It was a state of complete freedom and happiness. I knew I was "dead" and that I had the choice of continuing on from where I was or returning to my body and to life. I learned that no one judges us but ourselves, because I experienced the result of every thought, word and deed of my life, how I made others feel, my effect on the planet and all of life . . . it verified for me that there was no hell.[7]

Wherever we are in consciousness is what we'll initially experience on the other side. The masks we wear when we go across are the ones we'll wear until they're removed through an elevation of consciousness. This has nothing to do with Heaven or hell; it's all based on the law of cause and effect. We're our own experience. A depraved individual will find depravity; the judging theologian will find judgment; the believer in the duality of pain and pleasure, feast and famine, will superimpose that belief system over the truth of universal wholeness and harmony—until a change in perception occurs. And those with a spiritual consciousness will move with ease into the bliss of beauty, fulfillment, and perfect peace. Yes, we do have a choice, and the choice should be made while we're on this plane. That's called *preparation*—not for hell, but for Heaven.

The World Situation

I'm writing this chapter several months before the publication date for the book, and who knows what will be happening in the world by then. But if there's fear in your heart as you're reading this, then you've taken on a misqualified energy that will screen out the truth that *nothing is too good to be true*. Yes, what happened on September 11, 2001, is etched deeply in our collective consciousness, yet in the *11th* verse of the World Healing Meditation we read:

> *Let peace come forth in every mind.*
> *Let love flow forth from every heart.*
> *Let forgiveness reign in every soul.*
> *Let understanding be the common bond.*

Also recall Lesson 25 in *The Jesus Code:* "Pray not to change the course of events or the cause of conflict will not be revealed, nor display reactive interference, for life must be played as projected by the collective mind, otherwise the just end will only be delayed."[8]

We understand that the problems of this world must be solved on the level of consciousness where they originate—until there is sufficient light to dispel the darkness. And that's our role—to release the Light from within to do its mighty work, seeing only peace. Through our coming together in spiritual consciousness, the activity of Spirit will positively influence the leaders of every government, every religion, and the population of the world itself.

What is there to fear? Nothing. We step out in faith and *let peace come forth in every mind,* and we go about our business fearlessly. Can we not trust omnipotence? And we do what we have to do to quell the ego-emotion of anger. We *let love flow forth from every heart,* following the command to "love one another" without exception. We must also understand that in God, and in God's expression AS us, there is no unforgiveness, no resentment, no judgment. And if we're not forgiving in our personal sense of self, we're shutting off the divine currents, turning off the light shining from within, which means that we're useless in the cosmic scheme of things. *Let forgiveness reign in every soul.*

Finally, we *let understanding be the common bond.* And what is understanding? It is the practice of harmlessness in mind, heart, and action as we understand that we are all one, and that which we cast upon another will always return to us in kind. What kind of return do we want? As the Dalai Lama wrote via e-mail shortly after September 11:

> *A central teaching in most spiritual traditions is: What you wish to experience, provide for another. Look to see, now, what it is you wish to experience—in your own life, and in this world. Then see if there is another for whom you may be the source of that. If you wish to experience peace, provide peace for another. If you wish to know that you are safe, cause others to know that they are safe. If you wish to better understand seemingly incomprehensible things, help another to better understand. If you wish to heal your own sadness or anger, seek to heal the sadness or anger of another.*
>
> *Those others are waiting for you now. They are looking to you for guidance, for help, for courage, for strength, for understanding, and for assurance at this hour. Most of all, they are looking to you for love.*

Now that we've eliminated a few more blips in consciousness, let's . . .

. . . Reach Out and Touch Someone

On a radio show, someone once asked me to share the secret of how and why Jan and I have enjoyed such a wonderful marital relationship. I said that her happiness has always been my priority, and my happiness has been hers. There's a giving and receiving of unconditional love, honor, and approval that forms a bond—not only of an intimate relationship, but also one of deep friendship and playful togetherness.

What if we thought of this happiness idea in terms of all of our relationships? What if one of our objectives in life was to be a completely loving individual—to lift up others with an eye-to-eye smile, a touch, an inspiring word? Do we have it in us to reach out to others without thinking about what we may get in return? Yes, we have it *in* us, but do we let it out with our lovemates, family, friends, acquaintances, and even strangers?

Love is such a misunderstood word. "Tough love" can be terribly counterproductive, and to criticize "out of love" is like saying arsenic is good for you. On the other hand, tender love heals, breaks through resistance barriers, opens hearts, and always returns in kind.

Example: One of Jan's early childhood friends, a woman she hadn't spoken to in nearly 30 years, lost her son to a heart attack. Jan heard about it and called her old friend to express love and sympathy. The woman was so delighted to hear from Jan that she quickly passed over the death of her son and began to tell Jan how much she loved her. She remembered their sweet times as children, and had bought Jan's book *The Other Side of Death* and loved it. She also said she was surprised to see us on the Geraldo Rivera Christmas show to talk about angels; she'd enjoyed it so much that she called New York to order a videotape of the show.

What began as a simple reaching out with love to someone experiencing grief resulted in an outpouring of love in return—and the rekindling of an old friendship. Is there someone from your past who would appreciate a love-lift from you? Jan and I believe that when we reach out and touch someone, for the joy of it and without any hidden agenda, the law of compensation immediately swings into action, and we receive so much more than we've given.

I know that it's difficult to feel love for everyone, particularly if you judge only by the masks they're wearing. And this may include a family member, co-worker, or someone you don't even know personally. This is where the two-pronged approach of saluting the Spirit within them while practicing divine indifference comes in. You love the reality of that person because it is you, but you don't let yourself become attached to his/her mind-set, opinions, and prejudices. You let them have their own experiences without judgment. That's spiritual detachment.

I shared something in a letter to a friend recently. I was trying to make a point on inclusiveness and referred to a passage in the book *Tuesdays with Morrie*. Morrie the professor was speaking to the author of the book, Mitch Albom. He said:

> The problem, Mitch, is that we don't believe we are as much alike as we are. Whites and Blacks, Catholics and Protestants, men and women. If we saw each other as more alike, we might be very eager to join in one big human family in this world, and to care about that family the way we care about our own. . . . We all have the same beginning—birth—and we all have the same end—death. So how different can we be? Invest in people. Build a little community of those you love and who love you.[9]

To "invest in people" is to share yourself with others—to love, to reach out, to spread joy, smile, touch. Can we do that with someone who least expects it, maybe once a day? It's a giving and receiving, and opens up a beautiful two-way street.

Love can also be equated with *helpfulness*, if the help that's offered has no strings attached. It can be a little thing, a tiny positive blip on the universal radar, but it counts. I once noticed a small man trying desperately to reach the items on the top of the grocery shelf, so I gave him a longer arm and then followed him down the aisle to provide assistance a few more times. Later Jan helped an elderly woman lift heavy items from her grocery cart when she saw the woman was having difficulty. No big deal, but there were a lot of smiles, laughter, and kind words.

WHAT YOU CAST UPON THE WATERS RETURNS TO YOU. One time, I called a man to trim a tree that was rubbing on our roof. He spent over an hour cutting several branches, and when it was time to pay him, he said, "It's Christmas Eve, no charge, my gift." Neat.

Here's another example from my book, *Living a Life of Joy:*

> Jan was on a radio show in San Francisco, and upon its completion the producer called a cab for us. As we entered the car we silently showered love on the driver and asked him to take us to our hotel. On the way he asked what we were doing at the station. Jan told him and showed him a copy of her book. He asked, "Did you learn anything over there?" She gave him a brief report, and when we arrived at the hotel I reached into my wallet to pay the tab. He shook his head, saying, "No charge." He looked back at Jan and said, "To use an old expression, you made my day." I think the message of love from her book did it.[10]

I could go on, but I think you've got the idea. As Ageless Wisdom tell us, *"Love eventually perfects all that is."*[11]

CHAPTER FOURTEEN

Reminders

Here are a few reminders from this book that will help you become more fully aware, to understand, and to know the Truth that sets you free.

The one Presence and Power of the universe is individualized as me now. There is no separation between me and God, for I am God in full and glorious expression.

God, the infinite Consciousness of the universe, expresses Itself as me, as everyone. If Consciousness expresses Itself, what is Its expression? Consciousness. Consciousness expresses as consciousness, Mind as mind, Spirit as spirit, Life as life, God as God.

There is only one Identity. God is all there is. If it is not of God, it does not exist. I am of God, and it is impossible for there to be anything unlike God in, through, and as me.

I am the Allness of God in unique expression. All of God is where I am. God is what I am.

The only power is of God, and from the heart of Universal Being to the heart of individual being is the unity of Spirit, for God cannot be separated from God.

I am the Self-expression of my Universal Mind. As above, so below. God is in expression AS me in the physical world. As within, so without.

As God being me, I have the consciousness of abundant supply. It has been here all the time, waiting to be recognized. I feel the living flame of wealth in my heart and see it spreading throughout my world as perfect all-sufficiency.

As the Presence of God, I have the consciousness of radiant health and wholeness. This Truth stirs my feeling nature with joy and gladness. I know now that there is nothing to fear.

My personal self is the expression of the Spirit of success, and the consciousness of glorious achievement and accomplishment is outpicturing in the phenomenal world.

God is as me now, which means that the consciousness of love anchored in my heart is attracting perfect relationships to me. I let my consciousness be the mighty magnet.

I love the God-Self I AM with all my being, and I love the expression of my Self as me. The God of Heaven has become the God of Earth, forever one in Mind and Manifestation.

*I am the Light of the Lord, the transmitter of sub-
stance to create form and experience, the holy expression of my God Self. I am the Mind of Personal Identification, and I am blessed with the treasures of Heaven.*

*God is fully manifest as all aspects of my being.
God is my individual being, my reality. All that God
is, I AM. All that God has is mine. I am totally complete.*

*Within my Divine Mind is the perfect idea of every-
thing I could possibly need, want, or desire in this world.
I now look through Spirit's eyes and see the Holy Vision.*

*Guidance and protection are overshadowing me at
every moment. I am blessed with ideal relationships,
true success, the perfect body, financial plenty, and
every form and experience that would contribute to
blissful living. All that I could ever seek, I have.*

*As I keep my mind stayed on the Truth of my
being, the Holy Vision, all that is within my consciousness is eternally and easily being extended,
expressed, and made manifest in the phenomenal
world without any effort on my part. Forms of utter
delight are continually being revealed. Experiences of*

great joy are constantly pouring through my Self-awareness to be lived by me in pleasure and jubilation.

I dedicate my life to the Spirit of God I AM. I relax. I contemplate. I listen. I watch. The law of harmony is now ruling my world.

I acknowledge that Spirit has already provided for everything I could possibly desire in life. I have the Divine Design. I feel it anchored in my heart. That which I was seeking is fully expressed within me. Therefore, I have no unfulfilled desires. All is complete.

I see this total fulfillment as four patterns of light, the sacred diamond blazing in consciousness with the I AM Truth encompassing it. I see the great river of life flowing through my Divine Design. I feel its incredible rushing force.

I see the green diamond growing, expanding into a holy structure, beckoning me. Without hesitation I step into it and feel the electric fire. All false beliefs and error patterns are being burned away.

I am now clear, clean, and the river of wealth, wholeness, success, and loving relations is pouring through me. It is done. This dynamic energy is now moving to be in the outer what it is in the inner. I am a Complete Being.

I see change in my life as the natural order of things, as the breathing in and breathing out in the divine process of manifestation. I now fully accept change in my life, knowing that only my highest good is expressed in every upward circle.

I choose to forgive myself and everyone else in this world. I choose to forgive all negative aspects of my life as I perceive them. If there is anyone or anything I feel I cannot forgive, I forgive my unforgiveness and ask my Holy Self to forgive through me. I choose to be free of any and all resentment.

Divine Laws are the Principles of Being, the realities of life, the way things are in Truth.

The Law says that scarcity is against the Law, that abundance is natural, and that my finances are continually in a state of all-sufficiency. Regardless of appearances, I accept this Truth.

The Law says my body is whole, vibrant, and well, that radiant health is my true nature. Regardless of appearances, I accept this Truth.

The Law says my success in life is assured, that I am in my true place doing what I love and loving what I do. Regardless of appearances, I accept this Truth.

The Law says my relationships are warm, loving, caring, and meaningful, and that everyone I meet reflects back to me the true spirit of love and goodwill. Regardless of appearances, I accept this Truth.

*The Law says that what I accept, I will experience.
I have accepted my Truth of Being with all my heart
and mind, and I know that by Law, all that is good,
true, and beautiful in life is rushing to me now.
The Law is fulfilled, and so am I.*

*My conscious awareness of the Divine Presence as
my supply is my supply. I am now consciously aware
of the indwelling fountain of overflowing abundance.
Therefore, I AM abundant supply. My consciousness is
the very energy of money.*

*I AM the Spirit of Infinite Plenty. I AM boundless
abundance, and with love in my heart, I let the universal riches stream forth into perfect manifestation.*

*What is expressed in love must be returned in full
measure. Therefore, wave and wave of supply flows to
me now. I am wonderfully rich in mind and manifestation. I now realize my plan for abundant living.*

*In the Pure Being I AM, and with Thought Divine,
I speak the truth. I am the wealth of the universe in
individual expression; therefore, I am very rich. I
always have abundance, for I am the Law of Infinite
Plenty. I live the Abundance Ideal.*

*In the Pure Being I AM, and with Thought Divine,
I speak the truth. I am the wholeness of the universe in
individual expression; therefore, every cell, tissue, and*

organ of my body is in a state of divine order and per-
fect well-being. I always enjoy radiant health for I am
the Law of Purity and Perfection unto my body. I live
the Body Ideal.

In the Pure Being I AM, and with Thought Divine,
I speak the truth. I am the success of the universe in
individual expression; therefore, my every activity is
completely successful, and I go forth each day to
achieve and accomplish in accordance with my highest
vision. I am the Law of Victory and Triumph. I live the
Success Ideal.

In the Pure Being I AM, and with Thought Divine,
I speak the truth. I am the love and harmony of the uni-
verse in individual expression; therefore, I enjoy only
beautiful and loving relationships with everyone. I
have wonderful friends, the perfect life partner, and
totally harmonious relations with all. I am the Law of
Love unto my world. I live the Relationship Ideal.

There is always abundance everywhere, and I now
let it manifest in my life. I am open to receive. I can-
not be limited, for I am the Spirit of Infinite Plenty. I
am the Shining Sun of Supply, and God's wealth fills
my world.

I see myself with a magnificently healthy body in perfect order, where every cell is in the image of the perfect pattern. I am whole and complete.

I see myself as vibrant, energetic, and filled with a new zest for life. I feel wonderful!

I am enjoying the fullness of unlimited success, for I am the spirit of accomplishment, the force of achievement.

Every activity of my life now reflects only victory, beauty, and harmony. I live the Success Ideal.

Love is the greatest power in the universe, freely given to one and all. God loves me, and through God's love, I can love others.

As I love others, I am loved. My harmonious thoughts are returned in kind. What I am feeling about another, I am feeling about myself. I choose to only feel peacefully and lovingly toward all. I practice harmlessness in thought and feeling each and every day.

The I AM within is the identity of wealth; therefore, I AM Wealth.

The I AM within is the identity of wholeness; therefore, I AM Perfect Health.

The I AM within is the identity of success; therefore, I AM Success.

The I AM within is the identity of right relations; therefore, I AM Loving Relationships.

There is no lack. There is no lack of anything. There is no lack of anything, anywhere.

There is always plenty. There is always plenty, everywhere.

I am the open channel through which Substance is flowing as wealth . . . health . . . creative self-expression . . . as loving relationships.

All of my desires are now fulfilled in Substance. I relax in deep awareness of my Holy Self. I let go. I let it be done.

Let peace come forth in every mind.
Let love flow forth from every heart.
Let forgiveness reign in every soul.
Let understanding be the common bond.

PART II

Fruits of the Harvest

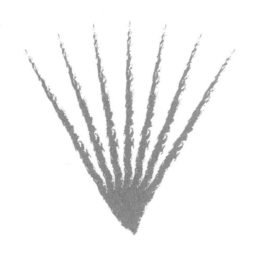

Introduction

A *miracle* is defined by *Webster's Dictionary* as "an event or action that apparently contradicts known scientific laws and is hence thought to be due to supernatural causes, especially to an act of God." To those on the spiritual path, miracles happen daily as Universal Love in expression, as the Law of Harmony in action. We may not recognize them as such—only a fortunate circumstance we might say, a wonderful happening, a surprise—but we should recognize and honor the Source. The Activity of God is the only Power.

My wife, Jan, calls miracles the "sweet mysteries of life." I like that. As I was writing this Introduction, she showed me a quote from Albert Einstein: "The most beautiful thing we can experience is the mysterious. It is the source of all true art and science."

Jan continued by saying, "Are we not all beguiled by the seemingly unexplainable happenings in life? There really isn't such a thing as coincidence. Prior to each event is a thought, conscious or unconscious, by someone, somewhere, within the vast atmosphere of Mind. And Mind is endless, infinite, and includes all that is and ever was." She then reminded me of the voice she heard in the car long ago. I'll let her tell the story.

When our youngest daughter was in junior high school, I was out doing errands one day, getting ready to turn into the local grocery store. I heard a voice coming from the empty passenger seat. It said: "Go home. Leslie needs you." Not accustomed to bodiless communication, I headed home without hesitation. It occurred to me as I was driving that my daughter Leslie was supposed to be in school, but I followed the direction I had received. As I pulled into the driveway, the phone was ringing. It was Leslie; an important paper due that day had been accidentally left at home.

While this may not be considered by some as a momentous life-changing experience, it's a good example of the Law of Harmony at work—for the good of all concerned.

IN LESSON 23 OF *THE JESUS CODE,* WE READ: "Normal is the ordinary, the expected, yet in spiritual consciousness one may see, feel, and experience that which is beyond the range of the normal." I comment on this in the book by saying: "It would not surprise me if a large percentage of you have had highly unusual experiences that could not be explained initially, but were later considered as part and parcel of your spiritual life. I know that Jan and I certainly have, and what we've learned over the years is that seeing beyond the range of the normal is a gift to enable us all to prove that we are more than 'human,' that nothing is impossible, and to demonstrate to us the existence of multiple worlds and dimensions—that 'life' is much more than we ever perceived it to be."[1]

My objective in Part II is to show what can happen when we commit to the spiritual way of life. It would seem that this decision lifts us to a higher vibration, one that offers us protective guidance, a shield of security, and a way out of lack and limitation, physical challenges, failure and futility, and discord in relationships. And in this process, we may experience hidden hands, unknown voices, angelic assistance, strange manifestations to alert us—or simply a new way of looking at life, which dramatically changes the outer scene. Even when we're desperate and struggling with life, we can be sure that the Lord is our light and salvation, as evidenced by this story I received by e-mail:

On a Saturday night, a pastor was working late and decided to call his wife before he left for home. It was about 10:00 P.M., but his wife didn't answer the phone even though the pastor let it ring many times. He thought it was odd that she didn't answer, but decided to wrap up a few things and try again in a few minutes.

When he tried again, she answered right away. He asked why she hadn't answered before, and she said it hadn't rung at their house. They brushed it off as a fluke.

The following Monday, the pastor received a call at the church office, which was the phone he'd used that Saturday night. The man he spoke with wanted to know why he'd called on Saturday night.

The pastor couldn't figure out what the man was talking about. Then the man said, "It rang and rang, but I didn't answer." The pastor remembered the mishap and apologized for disturbing him, explaining that he had intended to call his wife.

The man said, "That's okay. Let me tell you my story. You see, I was planning to commit suicide on Saturday night, but before I did, I prayed, 'God, if you're there, and you don't want me to do this, give me a sign now.' At that point, my phone started to ring. I looked at the caller ID, and it said, 'Almighty God.' I was afraid to answer!"

The reason why it showed on the man's caller ID that the call came from "Almighty God" is because the church that the pastor serves is called Almighty God Tabernacle.

Isn't it amazing how God works in our lives?

The stories that follow were submitted in response to an e-mail I sent to Quartus members asking for their personal experiences, happenings that document the truth that nothing is too good to be true. Let's look now at those sweet mysteries of life.

CHAPTER FIFTEEN

Phenomenal Happenings

The Angel in Blue Jeans
by Paris St. Michael

More than 20 years ago, my husband, Jerry, our two daughters (Julie, then age nine, and Debi, age six), and I were traveling along a desolate stretch of the interstate on our way home to Florida. Suddenly, a puff of steam erupted from under the hood of our car. This was long before the cell-phone era—we would have been lucky to find a pay phone at the rest stop that was just ahead.

Jerry parked the car in the first shady space at the rest stop. He got out and raised the hood, and as steam exploded into the sweltering August air, I sat there quietly asking God what we were going to do. Jerry's initial diagnosis was a split in the radiator hose, but there was so much steam that it was difficult to be exact. Unfortunately, there was no pay phone at this stop. Even if there had been, our car was German-made, and we had difficulty finding repair places for it, even in the large city we lived in. The chances of locating a garage with metric equipment and parts in this remote area were next to none.

I was trying to keep the girls entertained when I noticed a man headed toward Jerry. There was something more than unusual about this man—he looked like a fugitive from a stage play of *Grease*. He seemed to be in his early 20s, with strawberry blond hair that was slicked back in a '50s style. His clothes appeared to be spanking new: a dazzling white T-shirt with the sleeves rolled up, and stand-up-by-themselves stiff jeans with the bottoms turned up in a wide cuff. Who was this guy?

I looked around to see where he'd come from, but there were only a handful of vehicles in the parking lot when we got there; and one by one, people had driven those cars away. That left this man with no transportation at a rest stop that was miles away from even the smallest town.

I heard the man talking to Jerry but couldn't make out what he was saying. I began to get a funny feeling about him when he turned and headed toward the building. At this point, I got out of the car to ask my husband who his new friend was. Jerry reported that the man didn't give a name but said that he was a mechanic. However, when my husband had asked the man where he worked, he was very vague, sweeping his hand across the air and saying something like, "Over there."

Jerry told me that our blue jean-clad mechanic concurred that we had a slit in the radiator hose. He said it was on the underside, close to the radiator. Jerry added that the man had gone to see if he could find something we could use to carry water to refill the radiator.

"Mr. Blue Jeans" returned from the building and reported that there was an empty juice can that we could use. I thought it was peculiar that he didn't bring the can back with him. I stood near him at the front of the car and studied him more closely. I noticed that he never actually touched anything. He only talked, instructed, inquired, and pointed. He'd told Jerry only upon observation where the slit in the hose was. When the hose cooled, Jerry had to twist it upward to find the break, right where our mechanical advisor said it was. It could not have been seen without turning the hose!

I scrutinized Mr. Blue Jeans's hands . . . which were absolutely spotless. They looked as if they belonged to a well-scrubbed surgeon rather than a mechanic. I was getting more and more curious about our Good Samaritan.

Finally, Mr. Blue Jeans told us that if we had some electrical or duct tape, we could tape that slit, and it would probably get us home. We knew that we didn't have a roll of tape, but I had previously wrapped electrical tape around the handles of two tennis rackets that Jerry had shortened for the girls. I asked our spotless mechanic if he thought that we could take that tape off and use it on the radiator hose. He seemed to think that it would do the job.

Jerry and I each took a racket and began to unwind the tape from the handles. Then Jerry painstakingly wound the tape around the slit in the hose. That done, he headed for the building to round up the can that our mysterious new friend had discovered to carry water for the radiator.

Julie bolted from the back seat and ran after her daddy. I turned for a second to watch her. When I looked back again, Mr. Blue Jeans had disappeared from his station in front of the car. Then I caught a glimpse of him walking across the expanse of grass between the building and a dense wooded area to the left. I'd locked my eyes on him for only a few seconds when he suddenly vanished into thin air!

Knees wobbling, I climbed back into the car to keep an eye on Debi. I'd scarcely sat down when she asked me who that man was.

I told her I thought he was an angel, still trying to compose myself after witnessing his disappearance.

"You're silly, Mommy," she giggled. "Angels don't wear blue jeans."

A Change in Dimensions
by Patti Schulle

When my family lived in Pueblo, Colorado, we'd have to go out of our subdivision and onto a highway to get anywhere. One day I was on my way to the mall and grocery store. I was waiting at the stop sign and watching unending lines of traffic from both directions on the highway. My first thought was, Help! I need to get out and finish my errands before the children get home from school. *At that point, a lovely face popped briefly into my mind's eye, and a click sounded in my head. Suddenly everything changed. Only a couple of cars went by in each direction—and there was nothing else on the road. I said a small prayer and drove out on the highway and into town. I arrived home in plenty of time.*

A few weeks later, I was waiting for a green light outside of the mall. There were a multitude of cars going in all directions, as well as a steady stream coming off the interstate. That little click sounded again, and all at once there were only a few cars around and only two or three at the most coming off the interstate. Since then, I've often wondered if there was a shift, a change of dimensions that provided the clear path.

On another occasion (in Billings, Montana), my husband, Bert, and I were heading toward a place on the west end of town. I was driving down a busy street when I noticed a white car at a stop sign on the cross-street. I realized that the man driving the car didn't see us, and I immediately laid claim to our time and space. There was a very different feeling in the air, which got even stranger when I saw the car come out and literally pass through the back of our station wagon. The man never saw us. We were invisible to him. It was an indescribable feeling having another car pass through ours. Of course there was no damage—the molecules of his car just moved through ours.

Nashville Miracle
by Richard and Ilse Lantry

In August 1986, the Army reassigned me to Fort Hood, Texas, and the family move involved a convoy of three automobiles traveling from Maryland to Texas.

CB radios connected me in the lead car; our two boys in the second car; and my wife, Ilse, with our daughter bringing up the rear. We'd just entered Nashville, Tennessee, on day two when we encountered a ferocious thunderstorm with heavy rain and wind. Traffic was heavy, and the route was very tricky—involving several lane changes and limited visibility. Right at the most critical moment, the windshield wipers in my car stopped, making visibility near zero. This was followed shortly by the awareness that the car wasn't running well. The need to stop was imperative.

Just at the moment when the CB communication was fading and the connections were critical, the rain let up and an exit came into view. I exited followed by the others, and as we arrived at a large service station, the car quit. All parties were safe! The station had a repair facility, and the mechanic, after a brief check, declared the problem reparable and the necessary parts were on hand. (What were the odds of that happening?) The work was completed in about an hour, and after a short conference on the next leg of the journey, we were off again.

After just a few miles, we came upon a terrible accident that had occurred about an hour earlier. There were between 20 and 30 damaged cars. Huge slabs of concrete that had been on a flatbed trailer were scattered everywhere, and there were many emergency vehicles all over the scene. Had the car not broken down, my family and I would have been at the exact spot where the accident had happened.

We've often thought about this string of events, and we're sure that the angels traveling with us kept us safe. We often thank them for their actions—the future of our family was rested on that defining moment.

Fish Market in Another Dimension
by June Campobello

I made a weekend trip to Oklahoma City with a man I worked with to visit another friend, who was giving a dinner party in my honor. My friend kindly sent my co-worker and me off to see the city while he prepared dinner. Our only assignment was to pick up the fresh fish for his famous Norwegian salmon dinner.

Around 6 P.M., we happened to notice the time. We were appalled: The fish market was closed! While driving back toward our host's home, we were frantically discussing our options—which were slim to none. I was especially upset, since this nice gentleman had visited my home on several occasions and had been so helpful. And here I was, his guest, and all I'd been asked to do was pick up an order at the market. I was in tears.

My co-worker and I rounded a corner where three streets came together, and there before us was a fish market that was still open. We purchased eight beautiful salmon steaks and went gleefully to our host's home. He noticed that they weren't from his usual market. The paper and the bill were unmarked—my co-worker and I couldn't remember a name either, but we told him where the place was and said that it must be new. Since our host's place of business was just down the street past that three-points corner, we were accused of having had too much to drink during our afternoon of sightseeing.

The next day we drove by that intersection, and you guessed it—no fish market. How do I feel about this? It certainly was the best salmon I've ever eaten, which might be attributed to my Norwegian friend's cooking skills. But the fact remains that somehow, in our desperate need, we stepped into a parallel world. It wasn't the future—the market wasn't unusual or remarkable. And it wasn't the past, because there was current equipment in the store. When my co-worker and I were finally able to talk about it, we just called it our "Twilight Zone visit."

Alternate Realities
by Tonie Bowden

August 17, 1987, was the Harmonic Convergence, the day I had an experience that was a major catalyst in my life.

I was in Mississippi with a group of about 20 people, in a camp owned by the mother of one of the participants. The camp was located on a lovely winding road with a lake at the focal point. The backyard overlooked the lake, which gave the place a feeling of peace and serenity.

There was an aura of excitement and joy as we formed a circle that August morning. The sun hadn't risen, the grass was wet with dew, and the air was fresh and cool. We began to meditate, and at that moment, I felt "at-one-ment" with everything. As I sat there on the grass, I connected with and felt the presence of my Quartus family, my spiritual family in Houston, and countless others whose names I didn't know but whose spirits resonated with mine.

After the meditation, which lasted about an hour, we discussed what we'd experienced. By then the sun had risen, so we enjoyed the beauty of our surroundings. Reluctant to give up the moment, *we finally rose to go to breakfast. It was then that I noticed I'd been sitting for hours in a live ant bed. Yet I didn't have a single bite, and the ants seemed completely undisturbed.*

This was my first conscious experience of an alternate reality—that is, two realities taking up the same space but separate. Perhaps the correct term is unified. *This was the beginning, for me, of experiencing many "alternate realities"—and I believe I consciously experienced them as part of the answer to my question: "Who, What, Where, and Why am I?"*

My Father's Angel
by Dr. Ronald P. De Vasto

Dad is the oldest of eight children. His parents, both Italian immigrants, moved to the Boston area in the early 1900s. My father was born in 1914, and he came into this world with a tremendous burden of responsibility. His mother was a devout and loving parent, but his father was seemingly dedicated to taking every woman he met to bed.

Dad had to grow up fast. At any early age, he worked in the family store, went to school, and took care of his brothers and sisters—not much of a life for a young boy.

One day my father's sister, Jean, came home with a bad report card, and my grandmother was fearful of what would happen when her husband found out about it. Jean was a beautiful little girl, with a wonderful curiosity about life at the ripe old age of eight. Grandmother and Dad decided to tutor Jean to help improve her grades. This was the start of what would be many interventions by angels in the lives of this family.

One afternoon in early winter, my father was schooling Jean in the third-story attic, and Jean was sitting on the sill of the open window. After spending several hours going over homework, they were both exhausted. *My father turned his back to Jean while talking to her, and when he got no answer, he turned quickly toward where she'd been sitting. She was gone. My father knew that she'd fallen out of the window, down three stories into an alley filled with debris. He ran down the stairs yelling that Jean had fallen out the window. Dad was filled with fear, knowing that his sister was dead and dreading what his father would do to him when he got home. He kept running and hid out for hours.*

In the meantime, my grandmother rushed out to the alley, panic-stricken and expecting the worst, and what she found is still talked about by the family to his day. There in the alley was Jean, sitting on a box—with not a scratch on her body or a wrinkle in her clothes. She became frightened only after she saw her mother in a panic. She said, "Mommy, don't cry. The lady put me here."

Later, after my grandmother regained her composure, she sat down with Jean on her lap, looking through a book of angels and saints. She slowly went through the book page by page, hoping that Jean could recognize the angel that put her on the box.

Suddenly Jean put her hand on a picture. In a solemn voice, she said, "That's the lady, Mommy. That's the lady who took me out of the window and put me on the box."

The single picture on the page was the ever-loving face of the Virgin Mary.

The Sailboat
by Jan Price

In the early days of a tedious sobriety, one of those special souls who find their way through Alcoholics Anonymous was spending a warm summer day at a lake. Invited to join a group of old friends to go waterskiing and enjoy a day in the sun, it seemed just what was needed to aid in the healing process. As the day progressed, ice chests filled with food and beer were brought out, and everyone was having a cool one. It was so hard to say no. Keeping busy and active seemed the appropriate action, and another turn on the skis was available.

Gliding across the sparkling water, a silent prayer for help was uttered. Suddenly looming into view was a beautiful white sailboat with the word Serenity painted on the side in blue. With tears streaming down, the words of The Serenity Prayer came to mind, and with them the courage to make it through the day: "God grant me the serenity to accept the things I cannot change, courage to change the things I can, and wisdom to know the difference."

This precious one said to me some years after this experience, "I am a miracle."

And that is so.

Prayer Works Miracles
by Sydney McCain

In the summer of 1998, I was moving my son and myself from Nashville back home to Houston. Because I didn't have a lot of time to make the move, I contracted over the fax and phone with a little-known moving company out of Memphis. They were the only ones who could promise to have all of our worldly belongings in Houston by July 15, which would give us just a few days to get unpacked before I went to work.

On July 13, when the truck and trailer drove up in front of my condo, I got a bad feeling. There was no company name on the side of the trailer—just white paint all over it. But I dismissed my misgivings and signed the piece of paper the driver stuck in front of me without even reading it. As the two men went about the business of putting our household of goods into the trailer, my fears *grew, so I called the moving company. I told the man who answered that I was worried because there was no sign on the trailer and nothing to prove that they were legitimate movers.*

I asked, "What's to prevent them from just driving away with everything?" He reassured me that "Jeff" was one of their best and most experienced movers and that he had moved people all over the country for them. And so I let the movers finish the job.

Over the next two days, my son and I drove to Houston. We expected to meet our movers at our new house sometime after noon on July 15th, but when we didn't arrive until 2:30 P.M., I worried that they'd be impatiently wondering where we were. However, the movers were nowhere in sight. At 3:30, I called the home office to see if they'd heard from the men. I was told that the men had called in from New Orleans with truck problems, that they'd get the truck repaired and arrive the next day. I was puzzled because New Orleans isn't on any major interstate highway between Nashville and Houston.

Three months later, the company had no idea where the truck and trailer were. They hadn't heard anything from the driver or his companion—and the contract I signed held me to the minimum reimbursement of $.60 per pound because I hadn't bought extra insurance. It also stated that the company wasn't responsible for the actions of any of its subcontractor drivers and that I had no legal recourse.

I was in shock for the first few days, but I did have the presence of mind to phone Quartus and ask for prayer support. They'd prayed with me so many times, and I had always seen positive results. But as the days turned into weeks and months, I grew increasingly discouraged.

Some time later, the company finally located the driver at his mother's home. He said that he'd disconnected the truck from the trailer, gone to dinner, and when he returned, it was gone. Then the company reported the case to the FBI, who entered into the investigation because it involved interstate commerce. The agent assigned to the case said that the driver had entered a drug reha-bilitation facility.

When I heard that, my hopes sank, but a personal counselor helped me let go of everything by giving me a good metaphor. She said I was like a trapeze artist: As I swung out on one trapeze, I had to let go of it in order to grab the one swinging toward me. I took this lesson to heart. I fully let go of any idea of ever seeing my things again.

About seven days after I'd heard from the FBI, I got the call. My trailer had been found, and all my belongings were still in it. The lock on the trailer hadn't even been broken. The FBI agent said that it had sat for several weeks in one of the worst neighborhoods in New Orleans. All I could see in my mind's eye was a group of angels stationed all around it, guarding it with the prayers of my loving friends and miracle workers.

Lost and Found
by Aaron Heart

Sometime after I arrived in Portland, Oregon, I realized that my wallet was missing. I began a methodical search of the car. No wallet. I took the car to a parking lot that was large and empty, got out a tarp, and proceeded to pull the car apart, right down to removing the backseat. I looked through everything very care-fully. No wallet.

I went to sleep in my car and had a lucid dream. In this dream, I was in the car, and I woke up to find my wallet under my coat on the front seat. I woke up for real and excitedly reached where I'd been directed. No wallet. So I sat in my car, still ringing from the joy of finding the wallet in the dream. I started to think, Why let the feeling go? Why not build an anchor and associate the potent joy I'm still feeling with the thought of the wallet?

So I felt the joy and increased it ten times over until it was profound. Then I thought, Wallet, feel joy, see wallet. I did this several times, accepted it, and went back to sleep.

Morning came. I woke up, opened my eyes, turned my head, and there, sitting on top of my carryall bag was my wallet. Hallelujah! An angelic chorus sang in my heart, and I felt all tingly and warm. My wallet had rematerialized from wherever wallets run away from home to.

Sylvester Returns
by Dr. Sharon Shelton-Colangelo

It was a lovely morning in my small community of Grey Forest, Texas, and I was taking a walk along a narrow country road with my daughter. The day before, I'd heard Jan and John Price speak about the reincarnation of their dog, Maggi. Their experience of finding her again had really made an impression on me, and I was thinking about it as we walked.

Almost ten years ago, when my daughter was a teenager, Sylvester, our beloved cat, died. I couldn't dream of ever having another cat. We often joked that Sylvester was half dog, half human, and half cat. He meowed in complete sentences and went on walks with me to buy the newspaper. Many people commented that his large, unusual bottle-green eyes seemed wise and eerily human.

On this quiet morning, I found myself thinking about Sylvester. And I began to retell the Prices' story to my daughter, now grown and my best friend. I told her that John had had a series of dreams that contained specific details that finally helped him and Jan locate Maggi, who had been returned to them as a puppy in a nearby city. As I finished the story, I realized that I had tears in my eyes, and in my mind I could see Sylvester's image: his long glossy black-and-white fur, his emerald-green eyes, his cute little goatee.

Then with a rush of emotion, I heard myself saying, "I'd give anything if I could see Sylvester again." Just as the last word poured out of my mouth and my daughter nodded her agreement, a little black kitten suddenly sprang out of the bushes and sat at our feet. My daughter and I were so amazed that we laughed nervously and just stared at the little fellow.

Without a doubt, Sylvester was back. I looked in that kitten's beautiful golden eyes, and there was the soul of Sylvester. I felt as if I'd known this kitten forever. He began to purr, that large motor purr that I knew so well. Even though I was certain that Sylvester had come back to join us, my daughter cautioned that he might be a member of someone's household. She speculated that we ought to leave him where we found him, but of course he would hear nothing of it. Every time we moved even an inch, he trotted right after us on his tiny kitten legs, just like a dog. He ended up following us almost a mile home, walking right next to my feet, just like Sylvester used to. Every once in a while, the kitten would meow in varying intonations as if he were "talking." These were additional signs as far as I was concerned.

Later, my daughter and I went back to the place where we found him. We talked to the people who lived there and found out that this little black kitten had appeared out of nowhere one day. That did it. I tried to name him Sylvester, but my family wasn't comfortable with that. So we named him Inca.

I love Inca. I love the way he carefully creeps into my bed at night, just like Sylvester always did. I love the way Inca gazes into my eyes as if we share a deep, mysterious secret. And I love the familiar way he greets me with a question mark in his voice as if to ask me how I am, what's up. I know who this beautiful black cat really is. Sylvester has returned.

*[**Note from John:** For the amazing story of Maggi's reincarnation, not once but twice, please see Chapter 5 in my book* Angel Energy.*]*

A Beautiful Gift
by Beverley Tisdell

It was a week before Mother's Day, and my parents were out working in the yard. Dad asked Mom what she wanted for her gift. Without hesitation, she replied that she'd like to replace her special Bleeding Heart plant, which had been killed by the extremely hard winter freeze.

On Saturday of that week, I awoke at 2:00 A.M., feeling terrible distress and anxiety. I paced the floor, not knowing what was wrong with me but aware that I was both sick and not sick. A few hours later, my sister called saying that Dad had died of heart failure. Allowing for the time-zone differences, his last hours coincided directly with the time of my distress.

Mother's Day came and went. Dad was buried on a Tuesday, and upon our return from the out-of- town funeral, we found a beautiful Bleeding Heart plant on our enclosed porch. There wasn't any foil wrapping, or floral shop or nursery card—no identification whatsoever. Mom asked every family member and friend, telephoned every florist and nursery in the phone book, but could never find the source of that beautiful gift. Mom says that no one else knew of her request. To me, it was obvious where it came from—and so like Dad!

The Skies Opened Up
by Edana Lane

Part of my journey in this lifetime was a two-year stretch in the Blue Ridge mountains of North Carolina. I was moving from one sleepy little town to another, and my rather volatile landlord became angry when I gave notice that I was vacating the apartment. He had a notarized document delivered to me ordering me to vacate the premises by noon the day of departure, or pay an additional month's rent.

A few days prior to moving day, heavy rains set in. How would I get a truck close to the building without getting mired in the rain-soaked ground? The day before, the rain was incessant. That evening about 10:30, I called Silent Unity to ask for prayer help. I needed dry weather until 3:00 P.M. the next day. After that, it could rain all it wanted!

Thirty minutes after I hung up the phone, the rain ceased! The apartment was vacated by noon, and the last boxes loaded into my new abode just past 3:00 P.M. Then the skies opened up again.

Divine Protection
by Charlie Heathco

I was coming in for a landing in Lurel, Maryland. I was trying to beat a big thunderstorm, and it caught me on final approach— just over the trees, maybe 300 feet off the ground. I was suddenly enveloped in total blackness, with the plane being jerked around so violently that when I grabbed the mike to ask flight control what to do, he couldn't understand me. I was unable to speak clearly due to having the wind knocked out of me.

*He said, "Pull up and turn southeast away from the storm."
Of course, all my instruments were skewed all over the place due
to the storm—I just remember shoving the throttle to the firewall
and putting the yoke in my lap. It was the only thing I could do,
yet I knew it was a fatal move. Almost.*

*The flight-control officer told me later that I flew over the
office at maybe 25 to 30 feet, so close that he'd had to dive under
his desk.*

*Somehow, I flew across the bay, over 50 miles away, landed,
tied down, and waited for the storm to pass. Then I broke into a
crying jag just thinking about it.*

If that wasn't divine protection, what is?

CHAPTER SIXTEEN

The Voice Divine

New Life on Roatan
by Edwina Doyle Dozier

I was alone in a foreign country, dying in a basement, and there wasn't anything I could do about it.

Only a few hours earlier, I'd been snorkeling on Roatan Island's West End. I was enjoying the sunshine in The Bay Islands of Honduras, grateful to escape the Kentucky snow for my two-week break from teaching school. What was a middle-aged woman doing alone in Honduras? Well, just as Thoreau recounted his reasons for retreating to Walden Pond, I had my reasons for washing onto the beaches of Roatan like so much driftwood. My younger sister had died suddenly, my mother had succumbed to a long battle with cancer, and I had undergone major surgery—

all during the previous winter. Call it the mid-life crazies, but I really wanted to experience life on an island.

I'd discovered the breathtakingly beautiful Bay Island the previous summer, when I lived for two months in a bungalow at Anthony's Key Resort. It was then that I befriended the affable Elba Rosa and her charismatic younger brother, Freddy, who lived in a small shack in the village of Sandy Bay.

When I returned to Roatan, I was the guest of friends and distant relatives—Ben and Alice Jones, who owned an opulent white house near the resort.

I brought Elba Rosa and Freddy with me to go snorkeling with another American who had owned land on the island for many years. A sudden rain drenched us on the dive boat on our return to Sandy Bay, and I discovered after returning to the Jones's house that the additional pile of wet towels necessitated doing laundry. I remember thinking how fortunate I was to have access to a modern washer and dryer.

Upon reaching the basement, my bare feet quickly alerted me to water covering the floor. It appeared that one of the village kids who'd attended my Christmas gathering the previous day had gone downstairs and had overrun a commode.

"This could be dangerous," I commented solemnly to Elba Rosa and Freddy. "Someone could be electrocuted."

Being intent on accomplishing the task I'd set out to do, I put the clothes in the wash and sent Freddy to fetch Richard, the muscular, dark caretaker who lived with his wife and four small sons in the house next door.

Soon Richard was deftly sweeping water, but when he opened the glass doors, he triggered the security alarm. As he scrambled up the stairs to disarm its shrill scream, I firmly grasped the dryer's metal handle. Like an electrified monster, it grabbed me in its powerful clutches and shot electrical current throughout my now rigid body. Immediately I realized what was happening. I was being electrocuted, and I was going to die. Someone would find my charred body, and I'd return to the United States in a body bag. I'd never see my daughter again.

In spite of the excruciating pain, I was aware that I couldn't see or hear . . . and that I'd stopped breathing, like a diver with a punctured air hose. What a stupid way to die, I thought. I was just getting the hang of this thing called life, and here I was being sizzled to death.

As my life story paraded before my mind's eye, the juices slowly drained from my body. I'd spent my entire life on a spiritual quest, vacillating between traditional religion and Eastern ideas gathered in India. In the face of death, I realized that I wasn't ready to part death's curtain, to step into the spirit world leaving all my unread books, unwalked beaches, and empty journal pages.

I remember thinking, So this is death, and I started to surrender, if for no other reason than to escape the excruciating pain. At that instant of relinquishing my tenuous touch with life, I heard a voice that gently coaxed: "Don't give up. Try to scream. It's the last thing you're going to have the opportunity to do in this world."

I called forth the last drop of strength in my rapidly weakening body, and emulated what I thought would be a scream, since I couldn't hear or even see. Then I passed out.

When I regained consciousness, I was lying on the cold, wet, tiled floor. Elba Rosa and Freddy were screaming and crying hysterically, "Miss Winnie is dying! Somebody help! Miss Winnie is dying!" And of course, I thought Miss Winnie was dying, too. I figured that my heart had suffered irreparable damage and that death was imminent. My right arm, bright red, curled against my body like a lobster claw.

I discovered later that Richard had disarmed the piercing alarm a split second before hearing my scream, which had sent him into action. Seeing me prostrate but still attached to the dryer, he intuited what was happening, and without hesitation scooped me into his arms, breaking the current and saving my life.

We discovered later that the house wasn't grounded, and others had been shocked by the dryer, although no one had been hurt badly. Richard, who was also barefoot, and I were genuine "live wires"—saving my life was not only an act of heroism, but a miraculous defiance of physical laws. A scar on my right thumb is the only visible remnant of my traumatic event.

After returning to my comfortable life in Kentucky, I severed my ties there and returned to Roatan. For three years, I used my education and writing skills to repay my debt to the island's people for giving me a new opportunity to live life unselfishly and to evolve spiritually.

Now, when the time comes for my transition, I shall enter that dimension without regrets.

Glad Tidings
by J. M.

My husband and I married late in life, and after three years we began to think about having a baby. Even though my health was excellent, at 43 years old I was closer to menopause than having my first child. One morning I woke and had a rather insistent Angel Muriel wishing to speak to me.

She said, "We have come to bring you glad tidings and cheer at this joyous occasion. Rejoice as your life now changes for the better. Fear not the changes that occur; we will be with you during this time. You are with child now. Be at peace with it. Perfection and beauty will result."

A few days later, we joyfully confirmed that I was indeed pregnant, but my family was far from thrilled for us. They voiced many worrisome concerns about possible risks of birth defects, miscarriage, and not going to term. As though in response to my concerns, Angel Muriel came to me, saying, "Peace be with you today, beloved one! We herald you with good news and glorious occurrences. All is well with you and the child within, and we bless and protect you. We guide and protect you lovingly, and in all ways as we watch over you constantly. We bid you great and profound love on this day and all days."

Six months later, after a near-perfect pregnancy and an unre-markable labor, Una Sophia was born, perfect in all ways. She has become the joy of our lives.

The Voice Asks a Question
by P. S.

I'd spent the weekend in Kalamazoo, Michigan, with a friend. I didn't want to miss church on Sunday morning, so I left my friend's house in time for the service. I was traveling along when I looked down at the speedometer. I hadn't realized that I was going at least 30 miles over the speed limit. Just at that moment, a voice said to me, "What would you ever do if you had a blowout at this speed?" Immediately, I put on the brakes and began going the speed limit. My hands were clutched firmly to the steering wheel as I wondered about the voice I'd heard.

Within five minutes of slowing down, I heard a loud pop, *and realized that I truly did have a blowout! I wasn't afraid, nor did I allow the car to go off course, as I was holding tightly on to the steering wheel. I listened to the whisper, and therefore, I was ready for the experience.*

The Twig
by Jan Price

John has a very simple but beautiful gold chain he's worn around his neck for many years—in fact, he never takes it off. One day he noticed that it was missing, and he had no idea when or where it had gone. He checked the shower, the clothes hamper, and other possible hiding places, all to no avail.

When I came home from the office, he told me that it was lost, but he assured me that he was okay about it and didn't have a sense of loss. I replied, "Well, it's not okay with me. You love that chain, and I want it back." I checked all the places he already had, looked in the car and then stopped. With great power, I spoke the words: "I call on the Law of Spirit now to reveal the whereabouts of that chain!"

Immediately I heard a little voice, asking: "Do you trust me?"

And my heartfelt response was, "Well, sometimes I do, and sometimes I don't. Why don't you prove to me that I can?"

At that point, I went inside to take a shower. As I was about to turn on the water, John said, "There's a toothpick in the shower."

"You didn't pick it up?" I asked.

"No."

I opened the shower door, saw the toothpick, and leaned down to pick it up. But it wasn't a toothpick—it was a tiny little twig, and when I picked it up, John's gold chain came up from inside the drain attached to the twig. It had been hanging there all the time, held somehow by a tiny little twig no larger than a toothpick.

In awe, I called John, handed him the chain, and threw the twig in the wastebasket. Then thinking I should keep it, I emptied everything out. The twig wasn't there.

The very next day, something came up that needed a solution. When I took it into meditation, I heard the words: "Remember the

twig." Then came the guidance on how to handle the situation.
I will always "remember the twig."

Julie's Angel
by Paris St. Michael

*Many years ago, on a clear but blustery March morning, my
two young daughters were begging to go out in the yard to play.
We were all suffering from cabin fever after several days of spring
rains. The problem was that I couldn't allow 4-year-old Julie or
21-month-old Debi out in our fenced yard unsupervised. Although
the yard was fenced, the swimming pool was not.*

*I told the girls that I'd take them out as soon as I finished mak-
ing the beds and putting the laundry away. However, growing tired
of waiting for me, the girls began to squabble, and I eventually ban-
ished them to their rooms and resumed my remaining chores.*

*Usually I had all the drapes open to the pool view, but this
particular morning I had them closed everywhere except in the
family room. Then, unexpectedly, I found myself standing in the
family room with an armload of freshly folded sheets that belonged
in the master bedroom. I was silently chastising myself for being
in the wrong room when I glanced out the glass doors to the only
open view of the pool and noticed that the water was stirring.*

*A voice seemed to whisper to me: "Go see why the water is
moving in the pool!" It was a peculiar mandate, but assuming it
was just a thought cruising through my mind, I told myself that
it was the wind whipping the water.*

*I was ready to head for the master bedroom with my sheets
when the words came again: "Go see why the water is moving in the pool!" This time they came with great intensity and
with the sensation of a hand pushing on my back, propelling me
toward the door.*

When I got close enough, I saw exactly why the water was moving. There was a tiny blond head bobbing just under the water. Laundry spilled onto the floor as I tore open the door and bolted outside. Julie was totally submerged in a vertical position, frantically flailing her arms and legs. Her long ponytail was floating toward the side of the pool.

Without thinking about my actions, I stretched my arm full length, grabbed her floating hair, and pulled her to the edge. My heart pounded against my ribs as I dragged her little body from the chilly water. I bent her over to force water from her lungs, but miraculously, none came. Julie didn't even cough! She began breathing immediately. Too terrified to cry or speak, she just gave me a wide-eyed stare.

Little Debi suddenly appeared, crying hysterically, "Juwie go fimmin' wif her zacket on!" I asked her if she would go in the house and get me a towel for Julie, as I carried my freezing, wet baby to the porch and started pulling off her drenched jacket.

Debi quickly appeared at the open door, hugging an enormous beach towel that she'd taken from the linen closet. I guess she thought that since Julie went swimming, she needed a beach towel! Julie was dry and warm in no time. My nerves, however, did not recover so quickly.

Thankfully, Julie seemed to suffer no aftereffects from her experience. She went on to become an accomplished swimmer and diver, often winning ribbons in school swimming events.

I've thought about that chilly March day many times. Things could have turned out quite tragically had it not been for that angel pushing me over to the door and insisting that I go see why the water was moving in the pool!

Following Divine Guidance
by Doris Benitez

In October 1984, I took a vacation all by myself. I'd decided that I wanted to spend a week alone at some spa-resort just pampering myself. I picked one called Coolfont Resort in Berkeley Springs, West Virginia. It was a beautiful setting in the mountains and quite out of the way—at least for someone coming from Puerto Rico, which was where I lived at the time.

When the week was up, I was on my way to the airport and taking in the scenery, when all of a sudden I heard a voice within say: "You should move here." By "here," I didn't understand it to literally mean right where I was, but maybe the general area. It was more like a message to move—that I'd be moving "to" somewhere, rather than "away from" Puerto Rico. The message was very strong, but I still decided to take my time and give myself a year or so to plan it out, just to be sure that it wasn't a passing fancy prompted by the relaxing vacation. Also, I knew that I'd face some opposition from my family.

The seed that was planted then continued to grow . . . and it would not go away. All I can say is that I felt as if I'd been merrily walking down this road, when all of a sudden, someone tapped me on the shoulder and pointed at some other (a better?) road to take. I started thinking about where I could move to, and came up with Washington, D.C.—maybe because I'd been there before as a tourist and liked it, so it didn't sound so unfamiliar to me.

Over the course of this one-year period, I repeatedly told my family about my planned move so that they could become accustomed to the idea. Yet no one believed that I would really go through with it—that I'd leave family, friends, and a great-paying job to venture forth into the unknown, all on my own, and go searching for a new job and a place to live.

The time came when I knew that action had to be taken, so I set a target date. I went to speak with my boss to let him know I'd be leaving. When he asked me where, I said Washington, D.C. He asked if I had a job yet, and when I replied no, he asked me to give him two or three days to get back to me. When we spoke again, he told me I had a job waiting for me. It so happened that he'd just received approval to open an office in D.C., and the person in charge there could use my services. Bottom line is that not only did I have a job waiting for me, the company also paid my moving expenses.

Everything fell into place. I just knew that I was doing the right thing at the right time. Even my finding an apartment in a good neighborhood was divinely orchestrated. It felt as if someone had opened the door and rolled out a red carpet for me.

I've never regretted following that inner voice.

God Was Actually Communicating to Me
by Dallas Matthew Dahl

This experience happened in the summer of 2000. I'd decided to read whatever books happened to fall into my lap, and two weeks later, a book called Conversations with God *was sitting on my kitchen counter. I started reading it with the attitude of a skeptic, but the further I read, the more I realized that God was actually communicating to me through this medium.*

I couldn't put the book down, and as I was nearing the end, God started saying: "I know you enjoyed this conversation, and you are already starting to miss me, aren't you? But you must realize that I am always with you. I am in the poem you wrote yesterday, and I am in the next sentence your loved one will say to you."

At that point, my girlfriend, who was in a deep sleep, said, "You still don't get it." I tried to wake her and ask what she meant, but I thought that she might be mad at me for reading so late. But then I read the last sentence of the book again and realized that God had spoken through her to me. Then the voice said: *"I will always speak to you; it's up to you to listen. I can communicate any way at any time."*

That was the beginning of a beautiful friendship between me and the Most High.

Ask a Question and Get an Answer
by Mike Lewis

It was 1969: I was 20 years old and had been discharged from the Marine Corps just three months earlier. I'd already held two jobs and hated them both. I was a high school dropout with a GED and no promising job opportunities, and I was extremely frustrated.

I asked myself with great intensity: "What am I going to do with the rest of my life?" At that very moment, an advertisement came on the radio. A man's voice said, "Are you a veteran with a GED?" It got my attention in full. The ad went on to say that South Texas Junior College had programs designed for vets with a GED. The rest is history. I started at South Texas in the fall of 1969. In 1978, I graduated from the University of Texas Dental Branch at Houston.

I asked a question, I got an answer.

Conscious Contact with the Source of All Things
by Guy Paul

I was once an atheist. My assurance of the nonexistence of any sort of Great Spirit was complete. My life was run on self-will. The reaction elicited from me by anyone who spoke of faith was that they were a mental midget and should simply take a look at what's occurring in Bosnia or the Middle East and try to sell their "product" to those people. There were too many unacceptable issues in the world to be in a mode of acceptance.

It also seemed, coincidentally, that I was too sensitive an individual to live life on life's terms. Life was not bearable alone; there was no possibility of Fourth-Dimensional aid. Resentment and self-pity were constant companions. I drank so that I wouldn't care so much. Over the years, alcohol became my best friend and comfort. Gradually I forfeited my life a piece at a time for the comfort and insouciance drinking blessed me with every day. But as time drew out, my insouciance was forfeited along with everything else in my life. I was no longer free. Even with my drinking, terrible bouts of depression and despair froze me. It seemed I couldn't move, and pride and ego didn't permit me to seek aid from people. Prayers of petition were of course out of the question.

I wanted out of life. Suicidal thoughts were my constant companion. One day in a fit of self-pity and despair, I held a pistol to my head, thinking of the relief of death would afford me. As I held the gun, the thought came to me: "What if God exists?" And then the second thought came, "This suicide would be a ridiculous waste if that were so."

Where did those thoughts come from? I don't know, but I didn't find it necessary to shoot myself. This first epiphany is what I call my initial conscious contact with the Source of All Things. An accident? I think not. It was my wake-up call.

Today, my pride and ego are right-sized, that is, significantly diminished; and the miracle has happened for me. What has occurred is this: A primitive, seminal searching for my source has displaced the old dwelling in darkness. I am free. I have choices. I choose life. I choose light. I choose love, and I choose prayer and thoughtfulness. I choose to seek through daily meditation a conscious contact with the source of all things, which I AM an integral part of, from the beginning of time.

◎ ◎ ◎ ◎ ◎

CHAPTER SEVENTEEN
All-Sufficiency

God Is Truly the Sender
by Nohea George

It was August, and I was getting together the tuition for my daughter's first semester at school. I was short $372. I called my very close spiritual friend, who contacted our prayer group. This was Thursday afternoon. The first semester's tuition was due the following Tuesday. We all prayed.

On Monday morning, my son called me at work. "Mom, there's an envelope that just came from the Department of the Treasury, and it looks as though it has a check in it."

"Open it," I said.

"Mom, there's a check for $372 in this envelope!"

I replied, "Thank you, God."

And my son said, "Why are you thanking God? This check is from the IRS."

Of course I had to remind him that the IRS is only the middleman; God is truly the sender. To show us that this was a true miracle, the check stated that it was a refund on my 1983 tax return, which the IRS had originally denied payment to me because they said I filed it too late. I'd missed the three-year statute of limitations when I filed my 1983 return in 1988.

Ask, then know that your request is already granted.

The Power of a Child's Prayer
by Millie Bonazzoli

For weeks my third-grader had been talking about "Transformers"—those large plastic robot dolls that could turn into cars. It seemed as if all the kids had them, and he was desperate to get one. I had a prosperity tape, so I had my son listen to it every night and told him to wish for a transformer. He thought this was ridiculous, but he tried the best he could to listen.

A few weeks later, I picked him up at after-school care, and the minute he got into the car he started in again about being the only kid without a Transformer robot. I told him that we'd stop at the toy store on the way home to price the toys, and he could choose the one he wanted so that when he prayed for it, he would know which one.

He was so anxious that I dropped him off at the entrance to the store, then parked. By the time I got into the store, he was frantically looking for me. He told me that a man had been looking for a specific action figure and wanted to buy it from him. Confused, I located the man. He said that he was buying a superhero set for his son's birthday and the main hero wasn't in stock anywhere in the area. My son said that he had one at home and the man wanted to buy it. I didn't believe it, but the man told me that he'd pay $20 for it. I told him to wait, that we'd drive home to find it.

Once at home, my son produced a clean, nearly new figure of a Thor-like hero. I called the store and the man was still there. When we got there, he was so pleased that he not only gave my son the $20, he also added another $10 for my time and trouble. Suddenly, I had $30 cash in my hand.

The Transformer robot that my son wanted was $29.95. He walked out of that toy store with his new Transformer that very day. I saw firsthand the power of a child's prayer.

A Way to Pay for It
by Genevieve Normand

I was in the process of selling our home in Texas and joining my husband in Alabama. It was a hot and humid day, and our central air conditioning went out. I called the repairman, and he suggested replacing the old unit. Money was tight—I had two mortgages and not a clue how to pay for the repairs. So I sent out a prayer: "God, give me a way to pay for it, and I'll replace the whole unit."

Within minutes my doorbell rang. A woman was canvassing houses in our neighborhood for a place to keep her two horses while they were building their home down the road. She noticed that we didn't have any horses on our two-and-a-half acres and wanted to know if she could board her two horses for the next six months. I explained that I was in the process of listing my house for sale, and that if she could work with a 30-day notice, she could board her horses on our property.

She asked how much the rent would be, and I asked her what she was willing to pay. We agreed on $100 a month. The cost of financing my new three-ton air conditioning unit was $125 a month. I figured we would save at least $25 a month on the electric bill. Thanks to this answer to my prayer, a new unit was installed, which also helped in the sale of the house.

From Nothing to Two and a Half Weeks on the Other Side of the World
by Jim Dixon

In the fall of 1983, I heard a presentation by Sharon Tennison, who had just returned from shepherding a group of Americans on a "grassroots diplomacy" tour of the Soviet Union. Their experience with Soviet citizens was remarkable! It wasn't at all what we'd been led to believe about the Soviets as enemies—that they were bent on converting all of us to Communism and taking us to war if necessary in order to accomplish that.

When Sharon announced that she planned a second tour six months hence, I knew at the gut level that I was going to be on it. I didn't know how, because my architectural practice in Dallas had been in a slump the greater part of a year and money was scarce—but I knew that I would be a member of the second "grassroots diplomacy" tour group, and I committed myself to that end. As has long been my pattern, I started praying for guidance on how to go about it.

Within two weeks, I received a call from a longtime friend for whom I'd done some architectural work in years past. He and his wife wanted me to come to their town to discuss an addition they wanted to make to their home. When I met with them, I found their needs to be fairly extensive. As they outlined their program to me, the idea of the desired trip to the Soviet Union came into my mind. I knew the work that would be required of me was extensive and would warrant a fee structure beyond what a simple addition to the house might have been.

When it came time to quote fee for the work, I not only set it high enough to guarantee my trip, but I also told them what was in my mind. They were delighted—to the point that my friend stated that he wanted to go on the tour, too. As it turned out, his wife's health prevented his doing so, but both of them enthusiastically discussed what such a tour would entail and were genuinely pleased that they could make it possible for me to participate. God is good! In one fell swoop, my architectural practice received a shot in the arm, and I was assured of the much-desired tour.

I did go on the tour, and it was a life-changing experience in every way. Everywhere we went, when it was learned that we were Americans, they opened their arms, their shops, and their homes to us. We became honored guests and were treated to the best they had to offer. We weren't allowed to pay for produce, which we intended to purchase in their open market; we could not pay for taxi service; they presented the ladies in our group with armloads of fresh flowers; they popped open their best wines at every opportunity; and they were open in their discussions about religion and about government policies on both sides.

These people expressed in every conceivable way a genuine desire for peace with us. Peace did come, of course, a few years later with the collapse of Communism. I'm convinced that that turn of events was brought on, at least in part, by groups such as ours that went to the effort of going over there and expressing unqualified friendship.

Growing Cash
by Doris Blackwell

I'm suddenly aware that my cash reserves are growing by leaps and bounds. This could be the result of my saying as I write each check, "God is the source of my supply." As I say this, I put three x's beneath the line for cents. For some years, I've been doing this, and I've really noticed the change in my bank accounts.

My Miracle Car
by Michaela Turner

I'm a schoolteacher, and in 1999 I was teaching in a very bad neighborhood in North St. Louis. I drove a ten-year-old Toyota with 150,000 miles on it, and everything was falling apart. After spending $500 on it, the exhaust system went out, and the front end needed a lot of work. It was time to buy a new car—fast. I couldn't risk driving my car even one more day in that neighborhood.

I drove my loudly rumbling Toyota with the cracked windshield and banged-up front and back fenders to the dealership. I walked up to the salesman and told him that I wanted to drive off the lot that night in a previously owned car with no money down and with payments under $200. Then I informed him of the bankruptcy I had just two years prior. Ken, the salesman, didn't see any problem. After filling out the paperwork, I drove off the lot in a green 1992 Saturn. Oh, man—it was even my color! Fabulous. That was Tuesday, September 7.

On Thursday, September 9, I received a call from Ken saying that the bank would not approve that loan because the car was too old and they wouldn't finance a person with a bankruptcy history on a car like that. I was disappointed, but I kept saying to myself,

"This is my good coming about." I kept a very positive attitude and thanked God. I remembered that it was the World Day of Prayer, so something wonderful must be about to happen. Ken told me to come in on Saturday and pick out a different car, no older than a '94 model.

Saturday came, and I brought the car back. Ken showed me a white Ford, a small compact model. My heart sank. Then Ken said, "We do have this other car that just came in. It's being washed up right now."

He led me to the dealer car wash, and there was a '94 silver Chrysler LeBaron convertible! My face lit up, and I exclaimed, "I'll take that one!" Within half an hour, I was driving off the lot in my new car. It fit me to a T. I looked fabulous in my new convertible, and I still didn't have to put even one dollar down. The payments were just a little over $200 a month, and I never worried about anyone in the bad neighborhood breaking into my car because I knew it was a gift from God. My miracle car.

My Biggest Miracle Thus Far
by Nancy Meyer

I had a rental house that I decided I wanted to sell. On July 2, 2000, the renter's lease would be up, and I was concerned that she wouldn't move out willingly. If this happened, it would cost me extra money, time, and stress. I realized that I needed to decide exactly what I wanted to happen. The present time period was April, three months before her lease was up.

I made a list of my desires on paper. I decided that I wanted the renter to move out willingly on or before July 2, 2000. I chose that she would leave the house and yard in great shape, and that it would look cleaner and better taken care of than I expected. I went on to decide how I wanted the house and yard work to proceed. The *interior of the house needed to be repainted, the roof needed to be replaced, and the exterior of the house hadn't been painted in 14 years.*

On my written list, I decided that the house would be sold before the work on the house would be completed, and that I wouldn't have to advertise or hire a Realtor. I chose that it would sell for $80,000, and also preferred that it would sell to the first person who looked at it, since I didn't want to spend a lot of my time showing the house. It was really important to me that I like the new owners and that they love the house and living there *as much or more than I did—so I added that exact wording to my written list. Last but not least, I chose that I wouldn't have to do any of the repairs or painting myself. I wasn't sure how this would come about since I had only $500 to spend, and all the painting and repairs would cost $3,500 or more.*

I put all of this in writing as an affirmation. The last sentence stated that it would all come together even better than I ever dreamed it would. I read the affirmation aloud each night for three weeks, and I did my best to let go of all fear and anxiety.

Fast forward to July 2, 2000. The renter called to say that she'd moved out and I could come to inspect the house. Upon arrival, I found that she'd left it clean, and it looked better than I expected.

The following morning, I called a locksmith to change the locks. He arrived in an hour, and while making small talk with him while he worked, I mentioned that I needed a handyman and a painter. He said that his brother worked in that capacity for an apartment complex. He was sure that he would do the work and asked me how much I wanted to pay. I mentioned a figure of $300 or $350, and he said they would do it for $300.

While the locksmith finished changing the locks, I puttered in the front yard. My next-door neighbor, Cindy (whom I'd known for ten years), came over with her six-year-old son, Michael. She asked if I was going to rent or sell the house. I said, "I'm going to sell it." She asked if she could look at it, and I told her to go on in. When she came out, she said, "I love it, and Michael has already picked out his room." She asked if she could show it to her husband, Carlos, when he came home from work, and what was my asking price. I told her it was $80,000 and that I would give her a new key so they could look at their leisure.

That night they called and asked if I could come over. When I arrived, they talked about how much they liked the house, and Carlos asked if the four ceiling fans and satellite dish would come with the house. When I said yes, he screamed, "Sold!" I then told them about the work I was going to have done in the house—a new roof, replacing some exterior boards, and repainting.

Carlos said, "No, I'll do that. I used to be a carpenter."

"What would you charge?" I asked.

"Nothing, after all you've done for us (letting them buy it with no down payment), I'll take care of that." I went on to inform him that there were some additional little repairs to be made on the inside, and that I'd already found a handyman to do the work. As I walked around the house showing them what was needed, Carlos replied to each item that he'd do the work himself and he wouldn't accept any money from me for it.

At the lawyer's office, they had another surprise for me. They insisted that the papers be drawn up giving me the yearly interest tax credit for filing with the IRS, until they paid the house off. On July 5, they signed the papers and the house was officially theirs.

I look back and see that every single thing I asked for happened. It came about better than I dreamed it would—quickly, and in ways I didn't expect. Everything just fell into place with no effort at all.

A Time for Miracles
by Krysta Gibson

It was November 1984, and I'd been studying metaphysics for not quite a year. Through a series of "coincidences," I'd been hired as editor of a small newspaper—even though I had no experience in journalism at all. One day I was driving on the freeway when I heard a voice say, "Move to Seattle and start a monthly New Age newspaper." I didn't consider myself "New Age," nor did I have any money to start a business.

After dragging my feet for several months, I packed up everything I owned and moved to Seattle. I knew two people and had enough money to live for a month or two. A new friend and I shared a house, and I started putting the first issue of my newspaper together. Six weeks later, The New Times *was born.*

Although the printer I was going to use said that they'd give me credit, at the last minute they said that they needed half of the money down. I didn't have it, but someone believed in the project and lent me the money. Every time I faced a lack and wondered what I was doing, something happened "at the last minute." Sometimes I'd open my mail box to discover checks—tithes from people who believed in what I was doing. I was so grateful I'd cry.

Later, as I was working to pay off the printer and keep publishing the newspaper every month, I was given a gift from an anonymous donor. The amount sent was exactly the amount I owed.

After growing The New Times *to maturity, it was time for me to move on, and I sold the newspaper in late 1996. I look back on those years fondly, as they were filled with miracles I'll never forget. That experience has given me a base of trust and faith that cannot be shaken. The universe truly is a friendly and glorious place, filled with miracles and friends—if only we're open to receiving them.*

◉ ◉ ◉ ◉ ◉

CHAPTER EIGHTEEN
Marvelous Healings

Calling Upon Jesus and the Angels
by L. C.

Every morning, my 12-year-old daughter, Kathy, rode her bike to school. One morning I felt uneasy, yet I shook it off as nothing. At nine o'clock I got a call: It was a hospital doctor saying that Kathy had been hit by a car as she was riding her bike. The first thing I asked was, "Is she alive?" The answer was yes.

When I arrived at the hospital, they were doing tests and wouldn't let me see her. I called my husband, then answered all the insurance-related questions. At eleven o'clock, I finally got to see my daughter. Kathy's spine had several fractures; they'd called in a specialist. Later, the doctor showed my husband and me the x-rays, and we were told that Kathy had so many severe spine injuries that she'd be paralyzed for life. I didn't believe it and screamed "No!" I called upon Jesus and the angels for a healing.

Kathy went through six hours of surgery and wore a bodysuit and a neck brace for three months. We never gave up on our faith—but most important, Kathy never lost hers. We prayed together daily and read inspirational books about life and faith.

She's now 13 and wonderfully well, a normal kid. I drive her to school every morning. Yes, it was truly a miracle, and I am thankful for it every day.

The Walker
by Judy Smith

I am a walker, a doer, and a high-energy person. I love the world around me. I love the earth and all its inhabitants, and I walk because I love to do what I refer to as "Judy's meditation"— time when I can talk to the God within me and straighten out the day.

One Friday afternoon, my orthopedic colleague and I were talking in the corridor of one of the larger teaching hospitals in South Africa, a place I worked and loved. I mentioned to my colleague that whenever I reached out to touch something, I received a jolting shock up my arms. I'd had neck surgery a few years prior, due to a fractured vertebra in my spine, and I just figured this was the result of having overdone it somehow.

"Let's take an x-ray just to be sure," he suggested with more than just a hint of authority. Within an hour, the x-rays had been taken.

"Please take these straight down," the technician said as she handed me the large brown envelope. She didn't appear too concerned, and I wasn't at all. It was getting close to going-home time as I neared my colleague's office. His door was closed, which

suited me fine. I slid the envelope under the door and shot around the corner, just in case he was inside. With the weekend in sight, I didn't want to delay my departure.

I arrived a bit early for work on Monday morning, yet the telephone rang as soon as I opened the door to my office. It was my colleague. "I need you down here now," he said.

I took a few minute to gather my equipment, then headed for the stairs. He was waiting for me at the door. I smiled and walked into his office. An x-ray was on the viewing box, and I could see that this patient was obviously in trouble. My colleague explained in detail what the problem was, and what would happen if the patient didn't get to the hospital fast. "One bump, one jolt, and this will mean paralysis," he told me. "And I don't think this is something I can do. There's only one person I can think of who can handle this. You need to see him right away."

It still didn't click for me.

He continued. "I saw you fall on the stairs the other day. Now I know why. How long have you been battling to walk?"

My heart jolted uncomfortably with the realization that the x-ray on the viewing box was mine—that I was the patient we were discussing.

"How soon can you be in the hospital?" my colleague asked.

By the time I reached the hospital, my legs and arms that had once supported me so well were no longer doing so. When the neurosurgeon arrived, he said, "I'm so sorry that it's you." I suppose it's a little awkward to operate on someone you know.

I'd go on to lose almost all of the vertebrae at the fifth cervical level, and the third and fourth cervical vertebrae would be fused. After the operation, my mother told me that I was supposed to be paralyzed from the neck down. She said, "They were hoping to save some movement, but the damage was so extensive when they opened you up that they didn't think they'd save much at all. We were told that you might be on a ventilator for the rest of your life."

I was back at work after three months, and no one can explain why I have such a normal level of function. Today, ten years later, I outwalk everybody I know in both speed and distance. I play tennis and can still beat my kids and make them run around the court. I'm now aware that nothing is impossible, aware that a great and wonderful force courses through me. Miracles do happen.

Thank God and the Many Angels
by Brenda Clark

In January of 1996, my husband's secretary called to say that Ross wasn't looking well and they were going to send him to the nearest emergency room. I met the ambulance but didn't notice anything serious. I joked that this was certainly one way to get attention.

The doctor examined Ross, and all of a sudden his eyes rolled back in his head, his body slumped over, and the words he was saying came out garbled. The doctor said that he was having either a brain hemorrhage or a stroke. I paused out of panic for a moment to think about how I could best help my husband, even though I was assured that the doctors were caring for him. I began making telephone calls to everyone I knew to get the prayer circles going. I urgently explained what was happening and that Ross needed prayer right now.

A few hours later, our doctor met me in Intensive Care. He said that Ross would be there for three days, after which we'd just have to see. He said he had a little hope. For a brief moment, I wondered what that meant. Although Ross was totally paralyzed on one side, I had absolute faith that God was with us.

I'd grown up knowing about "hands-on healing" through our church. That night I kept my hands on Ross and stayed deeply in prayer, allowing God's healing to flow through me. Knowing that everyone I called was also praying gave me strength, and I didn't feel so alone.

During the night, miracles took place. First, Ross was able to move his foot, then his whole leg, then his hand and arm. By morning, his sagging mouth was back to normal and he was talking coherently. This was our first miracle. Ross was moved to his own room the next day, and was released from the hospital at the end of the week.

He began recovery at home taking classes for muscle coordination. I also noticed that about once a week, he'd have a faraway look in his eyes. All of the people who'd prayed for Ross while he was in the hospital were given updates on his progress, and by the grace of God and their prayers, Ross continued to improve.

Our second miracle came when Ross was given a Reiki 1 attunement by two beautiful Reiki Masters. After the attunement, Ross came back fully in his eyes, and he hasn't been out since. He was able to work once again.

The doctor was amazed. He told us afterwards that he'd given Ross a 70-percent chance of dying and a 30-percent chance of being a vegetable. Is that what he meant by a "little" hope? Glad I didn't know that then.

Thank God and the many angels—and the Quartus angels— that faithfully prayed with me during this period. My husband has now fully recovered from the stroke.

My Miracle Formula
by Stephanie Montgomery

Our beloved five-year-old Doberman pinscher, Tosha, was diagnosed with mouth cancer. She had a malignant tumor on the roof of her mouth, and when they did further testing, the vet said that the cancer had spread to the entire roof of her mouth. Other than extensive radiation treatment, there were no other options available except euthanasia.

After crying, I started my miracle formula for Tosha—a spiritual treatment followed by visualization techniques. Within a couple of days, Tosha had resumed eating, which she hadn't done since we discovered the tumor. My husband and I both noticed an amazing improvement in her. When we brought her back to the vet, three days after the diagnosis, she was also amazed, especially when she examined Tosha's mouth and found no tumor. The cancer tests were repeated, and Tosha's mouth was cancer free. The vet said she couldn't explain this but was very happy for all of us.

Tosha had a wonderful, healthy life, which ended at the ripe old age of 13.

CHAPTER NINETEEN
Loving Relations

Trust the Process
by Patricia "Patri" Hildreth

I was 33 and single when I found Truth teachings (Science of Mind). It took me a year to see how little I really knew before I started studying seriously. After a few months, I wrote a treatment (a positive prayer) for my perfect mate. This treatment wasn't anything new, but I felt it click. I knew something had happened.

Three years later, when I was talking with the man who would become my husband, he said, "You know, I never would have met you if I hadn't joined the Navy." At the time I did the treatment, he was a commercial photographer in New York, but two weeks later, he joined the Navy. Ten months later, he was in San Diego, and in six months we moved a block apart.

I was always drawn to the apartment building he lived in, and he said he used to notice my little house and car. A year and a half later, I moved into his building—to an apartment directly across from him. However, I wasn't aware of him, but fortunately, he was aware of me. He saw me struggling with a box and asked if I needed some help. We instantly liked each other, but since there seemed to be several differences, I didn't think that there was much of a future. However, something within me said to start treating (praying) to see the wisdom in our differences because the relationship felt so right. I'd never met a man who was so committed in his feelings for me. No accident in that. I'd finally become committed to myself; he was just a reflection of my own self-love.

I share the details of what was going on during those three years because, to me, it seemed as if nothing was happening. However, a lot was happening inside of me. I was healing my false beliefs about myself while the "Universal Wonder Worker" was getting the stage set for us to meet.

We were married on July 13, 1985. It was the first marriage for both of us. It just keeps getting better all the time.

Six Weeks of Angels
by Diane Pope

Four days after open-heart surgery at the age of 40, I was pushing it. I'd walked several trips around the nurse's station every hour. I ate and drank everything I was supposed to. I used my self-hypnosis and hadn't had any painkillers all day.

My doctor arrived and seemed very pleased. "Feel like setting a record and leaving here tomorrow?" he asked.

"You bet!" I said. After all, as a nurse, the last place I wanted to be was in a hospital as a patient.

Then he said, "I'll have the nurse make the arrangements with the nursing home." Nursing home? No way! He explained that he wouldn't send me home to stay in my upstairs apartment alone. There were no other relatives in town.

My friend Lynn found me bawling my eyes out, and between sobs, I explained my situation. When she left, I became even more morose. "God, how could you do this to me? You said you'd never leave me alone and here I am." I knew better, but . . .

No more than two hours later, I heard a soft knock on the door. Lynn came in, sat on my bed, and handed me several sheets of paper. It looked like a calendar of some kind. Next to the dates were the names of people. Some I knew well—square-dance partners, fellow workers, an ex-husband. Other folks I'd been around, but never considered close friends. "What's this?" I asked.

Lynn explained that she'd spoken with the doctor who told her that I'd have to have someone with me around-the-clock for the next six weeks. She then informed me that Jim, a friend who was between jobs, would pick me up the next morning and take me home. He'd stay until after dinner when the "night person" on the list would show up and spend the night. Every slot for six weeks was filled.

Herb, an old friend who had been out of my life, took over the details of living that tired me out. Each person was so special, like a gift waiting to be explored. In the past, I'd always enjoyed the position of being the caregiver. Now I learned how to receive help from others. It was a lot harder than I thought, and an important spiritual lesson I needed to remember.

God must have been laughing. I'd complained about being left alone, and he sent me six weeks of angels to cover every second. Actually, since that year I've never been lonely. Herb and I will be married 13 years this April. When God hears our cries, he pours out his goodness until our cups run over.

Frank and the Monks
by Jan Mahannah-Moskus

It was a typically busy day at the church office in mid-January, a month and a half after my husband, Frank's, death. There had been constant interruptions, multiple administrative details to take care of, and more phone calls in a day than I wanted to answer in a month. *I'd just finished counseling a congregant when my secretary paged me to say that there was a monk on the phone who wanted to talk to me. Distracted, but curious, I answered.*

The monk said that he represented a group of Tibetan monks who were touring the United States. I had difficulty understanding him, but gleaned that the monks would be passing through Baton Rouge Wednesday night, February 3, on their way to engagements in Florida. He asked if we'd consider sponsoring a performance in our church, providing them with food and lodging for the night.

I tried to clear my mind of the fatigue and grief that had haunted me as I coped with the reality of my husband's death. If they came, we only had three weeks to prepare for their visit. We were already promoting a special speaker, Walter Starcke, the Sunday before the 3rd and a concert the following Friday night. It seemed like bad timing.

I said, "I don't think that date will work for us. Will they be coming back this way later in the year?"

He answered that he didn't know when they would be returning, and that February 3rd was the only date he knew they would be in our area. I was ready to say, "Sorry, perhaps another time" when my inner guidance said: "Don't tell him no until you meditate on this." *So that's what I told him. The request seemed to be quite reasonable, and he responded with, "Certainly. I'll call you in half an hour."*

I got up from my desk and walked around the room, then went into meditation. "What's this all about God?" I asked. There was an immediate reply: "Do you remember when Frank brought you home a surprise at two o'clock in the morning?" *I thought back over our 30 years of marriage.*

Years ago, Frank had played Russian music one night at a private party for the Bolshoi Ballet. I'd managed the Gaslight Bar in his absence and had locked up the building at closing time. We lived on the balcony of the business, so I wearily waited up with a friend for his return. At two o'clock, he opened the door and yelled, "Hey, honey, I brought you home a surprise."

The surprise he brought me turned out to be nine Russian dancers and one interpreter. My fatigue vanished, and I welcomed our unexpected visitors. Because it was after-hours, we lit candles instead of turning on the lights. We put on Russian music on our tape player and brought out chilled vodka with coarse-ground black pepper for our guests. It turned out to be a magical evening of shared music, dance, and laughter. When we drove them to their hotel at 6:30 in the morning, they told us that it was absolutely the best time they'd experienced in the United States. They said that the next time we were in Russia, Frank and I had to come visit them.

"Yes, God, I remember," *I said through tears triggered by the memory.*

"What does February 3 mean to you?" *God asked.*

"Well, it's the Wednesday night prayer service for the church . . . and it would have been our 31st wedding anniversary."

"How many people are coming?" *Spirit asked.*

"There are nine performing monks and one driver," *I responded . . . then I stopped as I considered the synchronicity.*

Spirit asked: "Can you accept that this may be Frank's way of saying, 'Hey honey, I'm bringing home to you and your congregation a surprise on our anniversary'?" *I thoughtfully reflected on the idea.*

When Geshe Lobsang Tenzin Negi called back, I said, "You are to come." And God whispered, "They need to stay at your house—all of them."

"And they're all to stay at my house," I told him.

That's how the famous touring monks from Drepung Loseling Monastery (the former home of the 13th Dalai Lama), who had recorded the soundtrack for the movie Seven Years in Tibet, *and who were sponsored by Richard Gere Productions and had the blessing of the Dalai Lama, ended up being my surprise 31st anniversary present. What a gift their church performance and presence in our home turned out to be!*

Before they left the following morning, I played them a tape of Frank singing a gypsy song so that they could align with his spirit. Then they chanted a blessing for him . . . and for my new life without him. Yet, how can I doubt that he is near?

Thank you, sweetheart.

I am now willing to accept the unexpected, unusual, and amazing happenings in my life.

There is but one Presence in this universe, and I am one with that Presence. There is but one Power, and that Power is good, loving, and benevolent.

Knowing this, I am ready to experience the wonders of life, the new adventures that contribute to a greater understanding of the mysteries of the cosmos.

I am prepared to hear the inner voice, behold the phenomena of hidden hands, and welcome the work of angels on my behalf.

I am open to the truth that nothing is too wonderful to happen, that nothing is too good to be true.

Yes!

Notes

Chapter One: The Secret of the Ages

1. Alice A. Bailey, *The Labours of Hercules: An Astrological Interpretation* (New York: Lucis Publishing Company, 1974), p. 5.
2. Ibid., p. 94.
3. Manly P. Hall, *The Secret Teachings of All Ages* (Los Angeles: Philosophical Research Society, 1977), p. CXXXIII.
4. H. P. Blavatsky, *Isis Unveiled* (New York: J.W. Bouton, 1877), p. xiii.
5. G. R. S. Mead, *Fragments of a Faith Forgotten* (Hyde Park, NY: University Books, n.n.), p. 535.
6. Ernest Holmes, compiled and edited by Rev. Carol Sheffield and Kenneth T. Lind, RScP, *A Holmes Reader on Meaning* (Los Angeles: Science of Mind Publishing, 1994), p. 14.
7. Ernest Holmes, compiled and edited as above, *A Holmes Reader for All Seasons* (Los Angeles: Science of Mind Publishing, 1993), pp. 16–17.
8. William Walker Atkinson, *New Thought: Its History and Principles* (Holyoke, MA: The Elizabeth Towne Co., 1915), pp. 23–28.

Chapter Two: The Missing Link

1. Walter Starcke, *Summer 2001 Letter* (Boerne, TX: Walter Starcke, 2001).

Chapter Four: The Divine Design

1. John Randolph Price, *Angel Energy* (New York: Fawcett Columbine/Ballantine, 1995), pp. 139–140.
2. Ibid., pp. 153–154.

Chapter Seven: You Are the Law Unto Your World

1. Emmet Fox, *Alter Your Life* (New York: Harper & Row, Publishers, 1931), p. 144.
2. Charles Fillmore, *Metaphysical Bible Dictionary* (Unity Village, MO: Unity School of Christianity, 1931), p. 396.

3. Ernest Holmes, *The Science of Mind* (New York: Dodd, Mead and Company, 1938), p. 271.
4. Emmet Fox, *Alter Your Life* (New York: Harper & Row, Publishers, 1931), pp. 3–4.
5. John Randolph Price, *Angel Energy* (New York: Fawcett Columbine/ Ballantine, 1995), pp. 113, 114.
6. Emma Curtis Hopkins, *Scientific Christian Mental Practice* (Marina Del Ray, CA: DeVorss & Company, 1920), p. 22.

Chapter Eight: Where Is Your Consciousness?
1. Franklin Fillmore Farrington, *Realizing Prosperity*. Quote is from original manuscript dated 1923, p. 12. The book was published later (Los Angeles: Wetzel Publishing Co., Inc., 1931).

Chapter Nine: Act with Bold Authority
1. Alice A. Bailey, *Glamour: A World Problem* (New York: Lucis Publishing Company, 1967), pp. 243, 631.

Chapter Ten: The Dance of Life
1. John Randolph Price, *The Abundance Book* (Carlsbad, CA: Hay House, Inc., 1996), p. 2.

Chapter Eleven: Let It Be Done
1. Franklin Fillmore Farrington, *Realizing Prosperity* (from 1923 manuscript), p. 8.
2. Ibid., p. 22.
3. Vitvan, *The Natural Order Process*, Volume I: Foundation Work/ Science of Semantics (Baker NV: School of the Natural Order, Inc., 1968), p. 18.
4. Franklin Fillmore Farrington, *Realizing Prosperity*, p. 31.
5. John Randolph Price, *With Wings As Eagles* (Carlsbad, CA: Hay House, Inc., 1996), p. 73.
6. Charles Fillmore, *Metaphysical Bible Dictionary* (Unity Village, MO: Unity School of Christianity, 1931), p. 517.
7. Ibid., p. 518.
8. John Randolph Price, *The Superbeings* (mass-market edition, New York: Fawcett Crest, Ballantine, 1988; trade edition: Carlsbad, CA: Hay House, Inc., 1997), pp. 110, 111.

Chapter Twelve: Lessons from Within

1. John Randolph Price, *With Wings As Eagles* (Carlsbad, CA: Hay House, Inc., 1996), p. 9.

Chapter Thirteen: Things to Think About

1. John Randolph Price, *With Wings As Eagles* (Carlsbad, CA: Hay House, Inc., 1996), pp. 23–24.
2. Emogene S. Simons, *Introductory Study Course in Theosophy* (Wheaton, IL: The Theosophical Society in America, 1967), pp. 46-47.
3. Jan Price, *The Other Side of Death* (New York: Fawcett Columbine/Ballantine, 1996), pp. 149, 151-152.
4. Barbara G. Walker, *The Woman's Encyclopedia of Myths and Secrets* (Edison, NJ: Castle Books, 1996), pp. 387, 389.
5. Alice A. Bailey, *The Reappearance of the Christ* (New York: Lucis Publishing Company, 1948), pp. 146–147.
6. Jan Price, *The Other Side of Death* (New York: Fawcett Columbine/Ballantine, 1996), p. 128.
7. Edwin Steinbrecher, *The Inner Guide Meditation: Mastering the Jungian Technique of Active Imagination* (York Beach, MN: Samuel Weiser, Inc., 1988), p. 165.
8. John Randolph Price, *The Jesus Code* (Carlsbad, CA: Hay House, Inc., 2000), p. 133.
9. Mitch Albom, *Tuesdays with Morrie: An Old Man, a Young Man, and Life's Greatest Lesson* (New York: Doubleday, 1997), pp. 156–157.
10. John Randolph Price, *Living a Life of Joy* (New York: Fawcett Columbine/Ballantine, 1997), pp. 106–107.
11. Alice A. Bailey, *A Treatise on Cosmic Fire* (New York: Lucis Publishing Company, 1964), p. 594.

Introduction to Part II

1. John Randolph Price, *The Jesus Code* (Carlsbad, CA: Hay House, Inc., 2000), p. 121.

About the Author

John Randolph Price is the bestselling author of 18 books on New Thought principles and practical spirituality. He is also chairman of the Quartus Foundation, a spiritual research organization headquartered in the Texas hill country near San Antonio.

For information about workshops conducted by John and Jan Price, and *The Quartus Report* published by the Foundation, please contact:

The Quartus Foundation
P.O. Box 1768
Boerne, TX 78006
(830) 249-3985 • (830) 249-3318 (fax)
E-mail: quartus@quartus.org
Website: **quartus.org**

Hay House Titles of Related Interest

Books

Angel Visions: *True Stories of People Who Have Seen Angels,*
and How <u>You</u> Can See Angels, Too!
by Doreen Virtue, Ph.D.

The Experience of God:
How 40 Well-Known Seekers Encounter the Sacred,
edited by Jonathan Robinson

Power vs. Force:
The Hidden Determinants of Human Behavior,
by David R. Hawkins, M.D., Ph.D.

7 Paths to God: *The Ways of the Mystic,*
by Joan Borysenko, Ph.D.

Sylvia Browne's Book of Angels,
by Sylvia Browne

You Can Heal Your Life,
by Louise L. Hay

Audio Programs

Connecting with Your Angels:
How to See, Talk, and Work with the Angelic Realm,
by Doreen Virtue, Ph.D.

Invocation of the Angels,
by Joan Borysenko, Ph.D.

Prayer and Spirit As Energy Medicine,
by Ron Roth, Ph.D.

There Is a Spiritual Solution to Every Problem,
by Dr. Wayne W. Dyer (6-Tape or 6-CD set)

Card Decks

Comfort Cards, by Max Lucado

Inner Peace Cards, by Dr. Wayne W. Dyer

Messages from Your Angels Oracle Cards,
by Doreen Virtue, Ph.D.

Miracle Cards, by Marianne Williamson

The Prayer of Jabez™ Cards and
Secrets of the Vine™ Cards, by Bruce Wilkinson

All of the above are available at your local bookstore,
or may be ordered through Hay House, Inc.:

(800) 654-5126 or **(760) 431-7695**
(800) 650-5115 (fax) or **(760) 431-6948 (fax)**
www.hayhouse.com

Notes

Notes

Notes

Notes

Notes

Notes

We hope you enjoyed this Hay House book.
If you would like to receive a free catalog featuring additional Hay House books and
products, or if you would like information about the Hay Foundation, please contact:

Hay House, Inc.
P.O. Box 5100
Carlsbad, CA 92018-5100

(760) 431-7695 or **(800) 654-5126**
(760) 431-6948 (fax) or **(800) 650-5115 (fax)**
www.hayhouse.com

Published and distributed in Australia by: Hay House Australia Pty. Ltd. •
18/36 Ralph St. • Alexandria NSW 2015 • *Phone:* 612-9669-4299 •
Fax: 612-9669-4144 • www.hayhouse.com.au

Published and distributed in the United Kingdom by: Hay House UK, Ltd. •
Unit 62, Canalot Studios • 222 Kensal Rd., London W10 5BN •
Phone: 44-20-8962-1230 • *Fax:* 44-20-8962-1239 • www.hayhouse.co.uk

Published and distributed in the Republic of South Africa by: Hay House SA
(Pty), Ltd., P.O. Box 990, Witkoppen 2068 • *Phone/Fax:* 27-11-706-6612 •
orders@psdprom.co.za

Distributed in Canada by: Raincoast • 9050 Shaughnessy St., Vancouver, B.C.
V6P 6E5 • *Phone:* (604) 323-7100 • *Fax:* (604) 323-2600

Tune in to **www.hayhouseradio.com** for the best in inspirational
talk radio featuring top Hay House authors! And, sign up via the Hay House USA
Website to receive the Hay House online newsletter and stay informed about what's
going on with your favorite authors. You'll receive bimonthly announcements about:
Discounts and Offers, Special Events, Product Highlights, Free Excerpts,
Giveaways, and more!
www.hayhouse.com